DESIGNING
DESTINY

Also by Kamlesh D. Patel

Book

The Heartfulness Way: Heart-Based Meditations for Spiritual Transformation (with Joshua Pollock)

Hay House Titles of Related Interest

YOU CAN HEAL YOUR LIFE, the movie,
starring Louise Hay & Friends
(available as a 1-DVD program, an expanded 2-DVD set,
and an online streaming video)
Watch the trailer at: www.hayhouse.com/louise-movie

THE SHIFT, the movie,
starring Dr. Wayne W. Dyer
(available as a 1-DVD program, an expanded 2-DVD set,
and on online streaming video)
Watch the trailer at: www.hayhouse.com/the-shift-movie

***

*Everything Is Here to Help You:
Finding the Gift in Life's Greatest Challenges,* by Matt Kahn

*The Real Life of Yogananda: The Story of the Yogi
Who Became the First Modern Guru,* by Philip Goldberg

*Secrets of Meditation: A Practical Guide to Inner Peace
and Personal Transformation,* by davidji

Please visit:

Hay House USA: www.hayhouse.com®
Hay House Australia: www.hayhouse.com.au
Hay House UK: www.hayhouse.co.uk
Hay House India: www.hayhouse.co.in

DESIGNING DESTINY

Heartfulness Practices to Find Your Purpose and Fulfill Your Potential

KAMLESH D. PATEL

HAY HOUSE, INC.
Carlsbad, California • New York City
London • Sydney • New Delhi

Published in the United States by: Hay House, Inc.: www.hayhouse.com®
Published in Australia by: Hay House Australia Pty. Ltd.: www.hayhouse.com.au
Published in the United Kingdom by: Hay House UK, Ltd.: www.hayhouse.co.uk
Published in India by: Hay House Publishers India: www.hayhouse.co.in

Cover design: Julie Davison
Interior design: Bryn Starr Best
Interior illustrations: © Sahaj Marg Spirituality Foundation, India

A version of *Designing Destiny* was previously published by Westland Publications 9789387894532.

Library of Congress Control Number: 2019943481

Tradepaper ISBN: 978-1-4019-6428-3
E-book ISBN: 978-1-4019-5930-2
Audiobook ISBN: 978-1-4019-5931-9

10 9 8 7 6 5 4 3 2 1
1st edition, September 2019
2nd edition, August 2021

Printed in the United States of America

You are the experiment,
you are the experimenter,
and you are the outcome.

Dedicated to all sincere experimenters.

What does destiny mean in the course of our lives?
What is fixed and how much can change?
How can we design our own destiny?

CONTENTS

PREFACE

I HAVE ALWAYS BEEN FASCINATED by evolution and destiny. In my own life there have been pivotal moments when life took a turn, where a decision has led me down a certain path. One of the most important turning points happened in 1976, when I was nineteen years old. One of my college friends, who would watch me meditate, asked bluntly one day, "What are you doing? Why are you wasting your time closing your eyes? I see you are always disturbed when you try to meditate."

I said, "Well, I am trying my best, but I don't know how."

He said, "Let me take you to a lady who will help you to go into a trance right away."

It appealed to me, so I said, "All right, let's go."

He took me to meet a very humble woman in her forties, who asked me, "Why do you want to meditate?"

I said, "It's my natural desire. I would like to meditate. I would like to travel all over India, learning about life, like the great sages and yogis of the past. I want to become like them. I would like to realize God."

She said, "My spiritual Guide says that God is everywhere. When He is everywhere, why not look for Him where you are?"

I continued, "I'd like to become a wandering monk and just disappear. I don't want to marry."

x | DESIGNING DESTINY

Then she said, "God is not such a fool to create two sexes if one were enough. Isn't it a good idea that spiritually oriented people also have families and contribute to the future of humanity?"

She went on, challenging fundamental beliefs that I'd held dear. Finally, she said, "Let us not discuss this further. I will initiate you into a system of meditative practices called Heartfulness."

Sitting for that first meditation session with this lady was the most amazing experience I had ever had in my life—it was so profound, proving to me that this system was right for me. I thought, "If a trainer of the system can transmit like this, imagine what the Guide can do!" (You will learn more about transmission in Part I of this book.)

The spiritual guide she spoke of was Ram Chandra—and now I was longing to meet him. But I had to wait. I could only visit him during my college vacation almost a year later in 1977. When I reached him in Shahjahanpur, I found him to be a loving, simple, genuine, down-to-earth person. His utter simplicity amazed me. Just looking at him made me wonder how there could be such purity in a person, such simplicity. His whole being radiated love. There was never a dull moment, even when he was silent, which he was most of the time. There was always inner communion, during which I could feel his presence. That was the beginning of my journey with Heartfulness and my Guide.

Destined to Be Daaji?

Let me ask you, the reader, a question: Suppose my destiny was always to become Daaji, the spiritual Guide of the Heartfulness movement. Does that mean my fate was completely fixed? Or could I have spoiled that in some way through making a certain choice?

That topic is the heart of what this book is about: How much of our destiny is fixed and how much can be changed? Now, I don't want to ruin the surprises along the way! What I can say, however, is that from a very early age, I was drawn to spirituality, although I was equally comfortable in worldly life. One of the reasons I still find Heartfulness so fulfilling is that it supports us to excel in both.

I am sure, however, that my life would have never been as it is now if I had not met Ram Chandra, who is generally known as Babuji. He is the epicenter of Heartfulness and the reason I am doing what I do today. One day, the world will know the contribution he has made to humanity, quietly, in anonymity, with the true humility of a divine being. His inspiration keeps me going and nourishes my life.

He was able to distill the practices of Heartfulness from all the yogic traditions so that anyone, anywhere, from any background, any walk of life, who practices them sincerely, may evolve to the highest limit possible for human beings.

There are still a number of people from various countries who met him and spent time with him in Shahjahanpur, North India, and during his travels abroad. All of them have been deeply transformed by their experience with him, and most speak of him as "the essence of pure love." Since his passing in 1983, the organization has continued to expand and thrive, and his simple, practical approach has continued to form the foundation of Heartfulness today.

What Is Designing Destiny?

There were two main catalysts for this book. One was a simple message that Babuji gave in his hometown of Shahjahanpur in January 1982. In it, he addresses the goal of life and our spiritual destiny. (You will discover the message in the right context later in the book. I don't want to spoil the fun by revealing it now.)

The second catalyst for this book was a series of seminars that we at the Heartfulness Institute held for youth in 2014 and 2015. I wanted to share with my young associates the importance of living a life of purpose, excellence, and higher destiny rather than living as a reaction to all the stimuli and demands of modern society. Peer pressure is rampant; the media and advertising companies prey upon youth shamelessly in our material world. Without the guiding principle of the heart, young minds may easily succumb to the environmental pulls of our current era, without realizing that self-mastery is actually a very simple process.

In this book, I will share with you what I have learned about destiny, and how our beliefs determine the relative importance of fate and free will in our lives. I will also share with you a set of simple Heartfulness practices and lifestyle changes that can help you to design your destiny. What we do today determines our future. What we did in the past has already determined our present. This is how we weave our destiny.

INTRODUCTION

Destiny, Fate, and Free Will

THE FUNDAMENTAL QUESTION about destiny has always been: What is fixed and what can be changed? Are our lives governed by fate, or do we have the free will to choose our destiny? There have been endless treatises and debates over thousands of years examining the influence of karma, of astrology, of the Gods, of the fates, and of free will on our lives.

Some people believe in fate while others think that free will and freedom of choice are our birthright. Most accept a mixture of the two: there is no absolute free will and no absolute fate. Life is lived somewhere in between these two extreme views. It is like genetics. There is a fixed genetic pattern defined by the human genome, as well as a flexible epigenetic component. The basic genetic structure is fixed, but our environment, thoughts, and emotions all affect the way our genes express themselves, switching them on and off. Like destiny, genetics is both fixed and flexible. Without this, there would be no evolution!

Each one of us exists in the dimensions of time and space, and we are constantly making our mark in those dimensions by forming impressions in our energy field, creating a signature, a personality, defined by a set of cognates—an individual character or blueprint of our future karma. If we could only remove those impressions, wiping the slate clean, then the karmic blueprint would be erased, removing our limitations and expanding the possibilities of our future destiny. The good news is that those impressions can easily be removed to clear the energy field and transform our personality and karma. Throughout this book, we will discover how this is done, and understand why removing impressions can totally transform our lives.

The Principles of Destiny

There are some fundamental principles that let us approach this topic of destiny in a very practical way. The first principle of destiny is that we can only change it in the present. The past is gone and cannot be changed. It is advisable not to stay stuck in the past, as it wastes precious energy, especially as we will learn to remove the impressions left by the past so as to erase the blueprint it has left. The future is determined by the present, by how we live now. It is what we do today that matters. Every day is a golden opportunity to design the destiny of our future trajectory in every present moment.

The second principle of destiny is that we create it for ourselves by our everyday thoughts—our wishes, what attracts us and repels us, our likes and dislikes. Have you noticed that some things attract us, while others repel us, and still others do not affect us at all, as they are neutral? When we like certain things, we attract them to our own energy field. When we dislike certain things, we think that we repel them from us, but in reality they affect us just as strongly as our likes; we just bind them in a negative way instead of in a positive way.

For example, hatred can lead to thinking about a person just as strongly as love. I once had to mediate a conflict among a group of people who were very upset about their group leader—she was behaving in an oppressive way, and people were very hurt. They came to me complaining about her, and I could see that they were spending all their time thinking about her. They were meditating on her weaknesses and faults! Once they realized that is what they were doing, they changed their whole approach, and things started to go in a much better direction.

Most of the time our thoughts are busy in this activity of likes and dislikes, even though we are not aware of it: "I really like that house—I want it!" "I don't want to work with her—she is too arrogant," "I wish I were like him—he is so capable," "These people look dangerous—it's best to stay away from them," "She is so beautiful—I want to look like her," and so on. We constantly form impressions in our minds by letting ourselves react in the moment with our likes and dislikes.

The third and final principle about destiny we will explore in the book is that we are not alone; we are all connected. We are not only designing our own individual destiny; we are also evolving together as a species and in communities. This is known as co-evolution. This can only happen when we first evolve as individuals.

Many of us want to change the world and our collective destiny through external means, such as politics, government policies, social causes, and grassroots movements, and all of

xvi | DESIGNING DESTINY

these have their place. But society is made up of individuals, and Russian author Leo Tolstoy once said, "Everyone thinks of changing the world, but no one thinks of changing himself." To change the world, we have to change ourselves first. To design the destiny of humanity, we start with designing ourselves first and then expand our radius to include others. A day will then surely come when together we are capable of changing the direction humanity is taking.

The Importance of Training the Mind

Unfortunately, most of us have not trained our minds to escape this wandering, reactive mode. Like autumn leaves falling from the tree, blown by the wind every which way, we are going wherever we are taken, without any direction or higher focus. When the mind is like that, everyday events determine our destiny with no active planning or forethought on our part.

So what can we do? Start by training the instrument that is going to design our destiny.

Imagine that you have a beautiful new Ferrari and you are so happy driving it everywhere, across wide highways, through magnificent country, on long road trips, exactly to your heart's desire. But you are so busy driving that you have no time to service it. So after some time, the car's engine starts to lose performance and eventually breaks down. Soon, the car is no longer roadworthy.

But why am I discussing a Ferrari? What is the engine's equivalent that we need to keep in good condition to design our destiny? We call it the mind, or the heart-mind, or the subtle body.

It is only once we "service" or "train" our mind that we will have an instrument capable of designing our destiny. This means regulating our thoughts to find inner stillness and clarity, clearing the clutter of constant emotions arising from the subconscious, and learning to access a deeper part of our human potential within the heart that guides us like radar does. And for this we need a meditative practice, which we will explore in depth in this book.

You may say, "I am perfectly happy as I am. Why should I change? What is wrong with my current destiny?" Of course it is *your* choice, and if you are happy, you may not want to change anything. But are you really perfectly happy? Think about it. If you look around you and deep into yourself, you will discover that we generally base our happiness on external objects or circumstances, so when situations change and sadness strikes, we are left without any inner tools to cope, like the Ferrari driver left stranded on the side of the road with a broken-down car. It is smart to train yourself to be happy no matter what is going on.

Think of it in another way: Is it a good idea to ignore the needs of your body until you have a chronic or terminal disease? Similarly, why wait until your mind is falling apart before looking after it? Why not keep it in excellent condition, like the Ferrari?

Shaping Our Fate: Where Is Destiny Taking Us?

The word *destiny* implies that we are going somewhere or toward something. If destiny is fixed, is there any need to have any personal goals in life?

But if we believe that *we* design our destiny, then we will set a direction with a goal. And what is it that we want in life?

The most common answers given by people from all walks of life and cultures are happiness, contentment, and love. Also in some of the greatest texts, like the Ashtavakra Gita and the Bible, what did the sages of old say? Ashtavakra told Janaka to practice forgiveness, simplicity, compassion, contentment, and truth so that happiness and love can be exposed as the core. And Jesus's teachings are also based on the same principle in the Bible.

And what brings happiness, contentment, and love? Perhaps for you, right at this moment, it is a wonderful relationship or a great career, children whose lives are fulfilled, or a comfortable lifestyle. But even if you have everything else, you know that without peace and calm you will never be happy.

When you go deeper into the subject, as we will do in this book, you will agree with me that happiness does not depend on external things or people. Things like success in our studies, a happy family life, a healthy bank balance, good friends, pleasure, possessions, and so on bring temporary joy, and that is important in day-to-day life, but they do not ensure lasting happiness. Why? They are all ephemeral; when they are gone, the happiness disappears too. And that is not a clever way to go about life—letting others determine how happy or unhappy you will be. So we need to balance this dependence on outer sources of happiness with something more enduring. To find lasting happiness, we need to look deep within ourselves. It is all about balance between the inner and the outer life.

Let's assume for a minute that we do have a calm, balanced, and happy mind. That is already a great achievement, especially in the modern world of busyness, stress, and short attention span. But is that our destiny, just to be happy and peaceful? No.

It is only a stepping-stone. It is important to know what to do with that still mind, how to use it.

We may strive for self-improvement in order to excel at whatever we do and expand our possibilities. Human beings have always done so. They have been willing to undergo struggles and discomfort to attain their goals. An Olympic gold medalist, a master violinist, and a small child learning to walk all know this. Anyone who has ever had a goal or purpose in life knows it. We struggle for something we want. Contentment is not enough. We strive to excel and improve in whatever we love.

Life is about evolution, and every life is an evolution of some sort. It may be in developing wisdom, skills, and attitudes. Inventions and discoveries are also about evolution. Even a life of failure and struggle teaches us so much and may lead to a future of growth. We can't judge because we only know in hindsight how our failures have brought wisdom. What we do know is that this instinct to excel and push past the boundaries into the unknown is part of being human. The very fact that we ask questions like "What is the purpose of life?" shows that we have this urge. *Homo sapiens* means "wise man." Even the word *man* comes from the Sanskrit word *manas*, meaning "mind." We identify with our mind much more than our physical body.

If someone says, "What is wrong? Your face looks terrible," you may be offended, but you will be more offended if they say, "You have lost your mind," or "You are so stupid!" Our ego is hurt more by an insult to our mental well-being. That is also why mental illness is more of a stigma than physical disease. Diabetes is more acceptable than schizophrenia, even though both are serious health problems.

In April 2017, the World Health Organization announced that depression is now the number one cause of ill health in the world. At that time, there were over 300 million people with depression. What is the implication of this? It means a vast number of people are unhappy and wish to find a more positive, joyful purpose in life. We have reached a critical time in human history when we need to address the complexities that lead to so much depression.

If we examine our situation, we find that on the one hand we let ourselves be pulled by the desire for wealth, possession, pleasure, contentment, and success, while on the other hand we also know that lightness, joy, and love pull us toward something higher. In fact, this instinct for a higher purpose drives many of our behaviors. For example, why is love so important to us? A person in love has a spring in their step, a mother's love is as important as good nutrition to a tiny infant, while the love between a grandparent and a grandchild is one of the most beautiful things to behold.

We search for meaning and purpose in life, for love and inner happiness, and this can be witnessed in many everyday behaviors. For example, why do we try to escape our mundane existence, whether by healthy or unhealthy means? Why do children look at the world with a sense of wonder? Why do adults still love daydreaming? All of these things are symptomatic of the search for an inner connection to a different plane of existence, the spiritual dimension, which is part of our lives as human beings. It is also very important in the bigger picture of our destiny during and beyond this life.

But how can we know how much influence can we have over our future? Is it already mapped out for us, or can we create a direction in life?

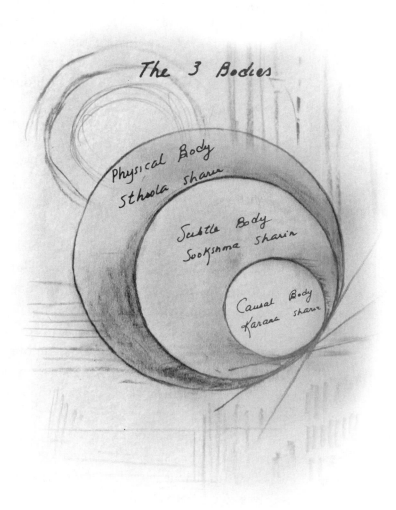

The 3 Bodies

Physical Body
Sthoola sharir

Subtle Body
Sookshma sharir

Causal Body
Karana sharir

What about Free Will?

Let's imagine that we can create our own futures. Is this possible in all aspects of our lives? We will explore this in more detail later in the book, but for now let's just say that we have three bodies: the physical body, or *sthoola sharir*; the mind, or *sookshma sharir*; and the soul, or *karana sharir*, and each one requires a different approach.

Let's take the physical body first. How much of it can we change? Some of us are short and stocky in build, while others are tall and willowy. We cannot change from one to the other, no matter what we do. We can optimize our body's well-being by healthy eating, regular exercise, good hygiene, proper sleep, and living in tune with natural rhythms, but the possibility of changing our physical structure or genetics is limited. Next, let's take the soul, also known as the causal body because it is the cause of our existence. There are two theories: one says that the soul is already perfect and changeless in nature, and the second says that the soul, too, has a purpose and that purpose is to evolve. Either way, the soul's evolution is not something we can control. It happens as a result of the practices we will discuss in this book. Nurturing the soul's existence is the way we support the causal body.

So that leaves the third body, the middle one, the mind, also known as the subtle body or the astral body, the energy field of the heart-mind. What can change here? Everything actually. We can train ourselves to regulate our thoughts, and we can work on our patterns and fears, our desires and emotional reactions. We can develop our decision-making ability, our generosity of heart, our attitude, our strength of will, and our capacity to love. These can all change drastically. This is the main body we refine in order to design our destiny.

How Do We Start, and What Are the Steps We Follow?

There are three broad steps in this process of designing destiny. First, everything starts from practice. This is the focus of Part I of the book. We need a set of practices that refine the mind so that it becomes an instrument for our growth. Such inner practices are known as meditative practices or spiritual practices. I will share with you the practices that have worked effectively for me—the Heartfulness practices. We start with practice, because change is always more effective when it starts from the inside out. Then it is lasting.

Heartfulness gives us a simple scientific approach to meditation: we are the experiment, the experimenter, and the outcome. Our heart is our laboratory. What qualifications and preparations do we need to start these practices? Interest, enthusiasm, and willingness. After purifying and simplifying the mind and heart, we are really able to expand our consciousness, realize our full human potential, and live a purposeful life.

Then, over time, practice leads to lifestyle, which is the focus of Part II. This is a natural and necessary step, because inner change is not enough; it must reflect outwardly in day-to-day life. What is the point of meditating if we do not become better people, kinder, more compassionate, and more giving? It will have been a waste. Ultimately, inner change and outer change cannot be separated, and our external habits and behaviors are the external expression of our inner state. So there is always a fine-tuning going on between outer behavior and inner transformation. As we grow and expand our inner potential through meditation, we need to refine our lifestyle. The two go hand in hand.

Finally, lifestyle leads to destiny, which we address in the last part of the book. This ongoing process of refining the personality through practice and lifestyle changes is known as the spiritual journey, or *yatra*. It is also known as the path of Yoga. By following this process, designing a destiny becomes second nature.

We create our destiny, step-by-step, bit-by-bit, through the journey of life. Every moment we make choices that lead us in a certain direction—either toward or away from our life's purpose. But it is not a linear journey, and sometimes we go backward to move forward. We make mistakes and learn from them, and that is all part of the rich tapestry of the journey. Every thought and every action contribute.

As our lifestyle evolves, consciousness expands and becomes subtler, to the extent that our ability to design our own destiny becomes natural and effortless. Now we shall explore that path together.

PART I

PRACTICE

It is not that meditation will give you everything,
but meditation done properly creates a condition,
and that condition will change you.

CHAPTER 1

WHY PRACTICE?

HAVING BEEN A student of spirituality most of my life, I have come to the conclusion that the purpose of any spiritual practice is to expand consciousness. The meaning of that statement will become clearer as you go through this book. For now, it is enough to say that Heartfulness practices enable our available consciousness to expand and evolve from mundane consciousness to divine consciousness, from:

me to we,
selfish to selfless,
reactive to responsive,
passion to compassion,
anger to love,
arrogance to humility,
anxiety to poise,
fear to courage,
contraction to expansion,
restless to peaceful,
imbalance to balance,
heavy to light,

gross to subtle,
complex to simple,
impure to pure,
desire to contentment,
attachment to nonattachment,
expectation to acceptance,
thinking to feeling,
feeling to experiencing,
experiencing to being,
and being to nonbeing,
intellectualizing to wisdom,
having to being—in love.

These changes are achieved through very simple practices, which we will now explore.

CHAPTER 2

RELAXATION

TAKE A MINUTE to observe yourself and see if you are fully relaxed. If you observe carefully, you will probably find that some part of your body is tense or uncomfortable. It is one of the modern-day epidemics; we live in a chronic state of stress.

Why is it important to relax? There are many reasons, including to unwind physically, to calm down when we are upset, to relax tired muscles at the end of a hectic day at the office, and to free our bodies and minds so that we can meditate. We need to be able to gently close our eyes and let our inner experiences unfold when we meditate. Arriving at effortlessness, combined with a steady and comfortable posture, prepares us to plunge into meditation.

That is why the first of the four core practices of Heartfulness is Relaxation. It lets us relax all our efforts. The Heartfulness Relaxation is derived from Patanjali's Yoga Sutras, with some improvements. When we begin, we focus first on the omnipresent energy, especially the healing energy emanating from Mother Earth. Then we imbibe that healing energy as it moves upward through our feet, allowing each organ to relax, each muscle to relax, each joint to relax. We proceed from the toes all the way up to the top of the head. And during this process, the Heartfulness trainer who gives the relaxation instructions will also connect him or herself with the Source.

When you experience this, you are touched by both the healing energy ascending from Mother Earth and the energy descending from the cosmic realms, doubly intensifying the relaxation process. You imbibe those energies, and when you then conduct similar relaxation programs you are able to create that same impact of relaxation.

You can narrate the instructions for others, or you can do them for yourself. The process is very simple and very gentle. If you are not able to remember all the steps and somehow skip one, there is no need to worry. The main idea is to relax yourself completely, to the extent of dissolving yourself and then bringing your attention ultimately to the heart, where you can intensely feel your own Center. That is the goal of relaxation.

Heartfulness Relaxation Practice

- Sit comfortably and close your eyes very softly and very gently.
- Let's begin with the toes. Wiggle your toes. Now feel them relax.
- Feel the healing energy of Mother Earth move up into your feet and ankles. Then up to your knees, relaxing your lower legs.
- Now feel the healing energy move up your legs, relaxing them. Relax your thighs.
- Now, deeply relax your hips . . . stomach . . . and waist.

- Relax your back. From the top to the bottom, the entire back is relaxed.

- Relax your chest . . . and shoulders. Feel your shoulders simply melting away.

- Relax your upper arms. Relax each muscle in your forearms . . . your hands . . . right up to your fingertips.

- Relax your neck muscles. Move your awareness up to your face. Relax your jaw . . . mouth . . . nose . . . eyes . . . earlobes . . . facial muscles . . . forehead . . . all the way to the top of your head.

- Feel that your whole body is completely relaxed. Scan your system from top to toe, and if there is any part of your body that is still tense, painful, or unwell, spend some more time immersing it in the healing energy of Mother Earth.

- When you are ready, move your attention to your heart. Rest there for a little while. Feel immersed in the love and light in your heart.

- Remain still and quiet, and slowly become absorbed in yourself.

- Remain absorbed for as long as you want, until you feel ready to come out.

Patanjali recommended relaxation as the prerequisite to his last three steps of Yoga: concentration (*Dharana*), meditation (*Dhyana*), and absorption (*Samadhi*). Unless your body is relaxed during meditation, your attention will keep moving from one part of your body to another as you try to make each part comfortable. If you meditate with crossed legs, your legs may become uncomfortable and your attention will then be on your physical discomfort. So in order to dissolve that, you need to relax.

When we experience relaxation, we really understand its impact, not just physically but mentally as well. It prepares us for what is to come at a spiritual level. Samadhi is our goal, which I would like to define as the ultimate spiritual relaxation.

You can practice Heartfulness Relaxation on your own every day, you can ask to be guided in the process by a trainer, or you can listen to an audio at www.heartfulness.org. Once you have learned the steps, you can easily guide others in Relaxation.

CHAPTER 3

MEDITATION

ONCE WE ARE able to relax, we can then meditate, which is the second of the Heartfulness practices. Meditation is often defined as thinking about one thing continuously, but we often get stuck with this definition and lose sight of the real purpose of meditation. Meditation reveals the true nature of the object upon which we are meditating. Such revelation comes not as a thought but as a feeling. Therefore, meditation is a process in which we shift from thinking to feeling—from thinking about the Divine to feeling the Divine Presence. It is a journey from the complexity of the mind to the simplicity of the heart. It is for this reason that many methods of meditation involve the heart.

In fact, most of us already know how to meditate. For a small child the object of meditation could be a toy for a birthday or a group of ants in the garden; for an adult it could be wealth, power, success, a loving relationship, or a higher purpose. When we focus our attention upon one thing, it is meditation. So it is the object of meditation that needs to be appropriate for the goal we want to attain, as the universal adage about meditation tells us: we become the object of our meditation, as a result of the power of our own thought.

Everything starts with thought. In Heartfulness Meditation that thought is "The source of divine light already present within my heart is drawing me inward." But it does not end with that thought, which is just a doorway into a vast inner universe.

We are used to having so many thoughts whizzing around in our minds. We are certainly not used to thinking only about one thing, so when we start meditating we are often disappointed by the number of thoughts that appear in our mind as we sit in silence. It is natural, and in fact, it is expected that different thoughts will arise. In Heartfulness Meditation we do not repress thoughts, feelings, and emotions. Left inside, they build up like the steam inside a pressure cooker, or they lay dormant waiting for an opportunity to germinate. They are better out than in. We want them to leave, and as they leave we often become aware of their presence. When that happens, we learn to ignore them as the mind lets them go. So the idea is not to fight with them, but simply remind ourselves that we are meditating.

But even Heartfulness Meditation will become like any other type of meditation without Transmission, or *pranahuti*. It is difficult to describe Transmission but easy to experience its transformative effects, so it is wise to approach Heartfulness as a scientist: first meditate without Transmission, then meditate with Transmission, and compare the two experiences.

Heartfulness Meditation

Here are the steps of Heartfulness Meditation, which can be done with or without the help of pranahuti.

- Sit comfortably, close your eyes softly and gently, and relax.

- Turn your attention inward and gently have the thought that the source of divine light already present in your heart is attracting you from within. Do this in a gentle and natural way.

- There is no need to concentrate. If you find your awareness drifting to other thoughts, gently come back to the idea of light in your heart.

- Let your awareness rest in your heart. Feel yourself melting into your heart. It is all right if you relax into a deeper state beyond awareness.

- Stay in meditation until you feel it is completed.

Let it be soft, as no force is needed during meditation. Meditate like this for half an hour to begin with and then, over a few days, weeks, or months, slowly increase this period up to one hour.

After completing meditation, sit for five minutes so that you can observe and savor the condition you feel within. Each time it is a unique condition, a unique gift. Hold on to it and cultivate that state. Slowly get up from your position, carrying that condition with you, as it has become a part of you.

Transmission

Transmission is the specialty of Heartfulness Meditation. Transmission removes the inner complexities or knots in our energy field so that the spiritual centers, or *chakras*, are cleaned and illuminated. Transmission removes the obstacles on the journey to the Source and makes meditation truly dynamic.

The Sanskrit word for Transmission is *pranahuti,* composed of *prana* and *ahuti,* where *prana* means energy or essence, and *ahuti* means offering or sacrifice: the prana of the transmitter is being offered, but to go on sacrificing or transmitting from a limited source will lead to depletion, so the person who is transmitting prana must be connected to the infinite Source so that they can go on transmitting. You can think of it as original, cosmic energy or divine essence flowing from the Guide into the hearts of seekers, much like a mother's love flows naturally to her children for their growth and sustenance.

If you consider Einstein's famous equation, $E=mc^2$, energy is always limited by the velocity of light and the finiteness of mass, but Transmission is not bound by physical laws. The instant Transmission starts flowing, a seeker receives it wherever he or she may be. If you merely think of Transmission, it starts to flow. Even light cannot travel instantaneously. If a distance can be traversed in zero time, the velocity is infinite. Hypothetically, what would happen to Einstein's equation if we were to substitute the speed of light with infinite, limitless velocity? Inserting infinity into the equation would mean that the energy that comes to us would also be infinite, and its source would also have to be infinite. That is Transmission.

There is another scientific principle that helps us understand the effect of Transmission, and that is entropy. Entropy is the measure of disorder in any system. In order to maintain a low level of entropy, there is the need for external input of energy into that system. Lacking such input or efforts, the system often disintegrates.

But not all energy input is stabilizing. For example, when we get angry, there is a greater flow of energy, but it destabilizes the system because it is working against us. So it is not only the energy input, but also the direction of the energy input. Compare two situations: in the first, attention is moving outward toward the periphery; in the second, attention is moving inward toward the center of the system. If our attention is drawn to the periphery, our system becomes unstable, whereas when it is drawn to the center, it stabilizes. In meditation with Transmission, our attention naturally flows inward, so our system becomes highly stable, leading to lower and lower entropy. And what is the center around which the vortex of our life exists? It is the soul.

Imagine a beautiful flower blooming in the garden. If you run past it, you will not be able to appreciate its beauty, whereas if you are walking close by, you can enjoy it more, and if you stand still in front of it, you will appreciate its beauty even more. If you are flying, then you will not even see the flower below you on the Earth. When we are moving rapidly, we miss out on many things.

The mind is faster than any physical movement. When the mind is moving rapidly from one object to another, one subject to another, one venture to another, what we miss is the blooming of the flower that is inside us. We not only miss out on the details, we miss out completely on the existence of the flower itself. That flower is our soul. Transmission pulls us so deeply into the stillness within that our attention goes to that flower. Treat it as an endangered species: How well do we look after this endangered species with love? Our undivided attention will ensure its survival, but our attention is often elsewhere outside. When we keep on moving, keep on ideating, keep on cognizing things, then we miss out on the inner beauty. What does meditation do? It centers the mind, helping it come to rest, matching the inner stillness of that sacred flower, which is steady and waiting. We try to match the inner stillness, the vibratory level of our soul, with the mind. Once this happens, something clicks. That is the moment of Realization—the absolute, perfect resonance of our outermost subtle body with the innermost sacred flower, when we are one.

Transmission conveys many meanings in various languages. For example, the first Guide of the Heartfulness tradition, Lalaji, wrote a lot about sound. He said, "Sound is the manifestation of consciousness. It is the life of lives, the soul of souls and the existence of existences. The whole world rests on it. It is the Absolute Base and the Perpetual Foundation of all creation. . . . Everywhere the vibrant currents of the movement of sound are found present in the form of Divine Light. Wherever there is movement, there is the current of sound." If you substitute "sound" with "Transmission," then what he says makes sense, because he is not writing about truck sounds and musical sounds, but about the subtlest vibrationless vibrations.

The Farsi word for Transmission, *tavajjo,* means "attention." The full attention of the transmitter is on the receiver. So it is a state in which the transmitter is very focused, with the spiritual goal of oneness with the Source in mind. That gives us another level of understanding.

And then there is another meaning: Transmission is love.

But then let's relate these various meanings to our spiritual journey. We are moving toward the Source, the nothingness, so how can we be one with that Source when we still have vibrations or even love? Transmission comes from the Source and touches the Source, so it must be the absolute essence of nothingness. It is indescribable.

We feel the effect of Transmission on the body in the form of relaxation, and we also feel some sort of detensioning or stillness in the mind. Emotionally we tend to become "zero"and feel balanced inside. Everything becomes quieter, and the subtle body comes to a standstill. No external sound can help us achieve this; neither can any inner sound from reciting *mantras* help. They all fail. It is beyond sound. It is beyond any mental makeup. No instrument can take us to that level of absolute stillness except the essence of that nothingness, Transmission.

The call of spirituality is change: "I must transform myself from whatever I am today to what I ought to be." What is it that is preventing me? The heaviness created by my samskaras, my impressions. How does Transmission help us to be free of the shackles of these impressions that we have been carrying from one life to another life? They are not something with physical attributes that can be removed. They are like wrinkles in clothes that have to be smoothened by ironing; the samskaras that create ripples in the mind have to be removed and somehow Transmission irons them out. We could describe the process as "magical," because it is something that cannot be expressed in words. Transmission goes to the very root of the samskara and removes it. At times, it allows it to dissolve or evaporate so as to bring the vibrations of impressions to zero.

There is a reference to the word *pranahuti* in the *Kena Upanishad*, where it is described as *pranasya pranah*, meaning "life of life." In short, it is the life-giving force. But we already have a life force within us, the soul. So the question arises, "Is the soul not self-sufficient in making our life?" Here is an analogy: during the hot summer months, especially in India, the leaves wilt on the trees. They sometimes appear as if they are going to die. The life drains from them, although the roots underground keep on absorbing moisture and nutrients to the extent possible. But with the first rains of the monsoon, the trees come to life. New life begins, there is freshness, and there is so much joy all around.

In the same way, we exist because of the soul that is within us, but the moment we receive the first Transmission, we absorb nourishment for the soul, life changes, and there is freshness in our existence. It is then up to us to make use of it in the best way, and that is where we all differ. If we continue the analogy of the monsoon, rain falls on fertile soil, on poor desert soil, and on rock, and each environment will respond differently to its life-giving potential. Likewise, each one of us responds to pranahuti according to our nature. When we are very receptive, when there is humility, when there is an emotional vacuum within, it pours in. We receive it, and it flows all throughout our system. Not only do we receive it, we are also able to unconsciously share it with others as the heart is saturated with its essence. Having received the Transmission, we can now distribute it.

There is no Heartfulness session without Transmission, and its purpose is multifold. Imagine a person who cannot walk. They need a cane, or crutches or a wheelchair. Similarly, when a person is unable to regulate their mind or traverse the various layers of consciousness, it is Transmission that prepares the way into superconsciousness—the vast expanse of the consciousness spectrum that is above the narrow sphere of consciousness. They cannot move even a millimeter in consciousness through self-effort. Transmission acts like a cane or crutch to support consciousness to expand into another dimension.

It helps us transcend from one level to another level, to soar higher into superconsciousness and dive deeper, cleaning the subconscious depths of the mind. That is its primary role.

We receive the essence of Transmission in the first meditation session so that the Source can work its magic. When we compare meditation without Transmission to Heartfulness Meditation with Transmission and feel the difference, we are recognizing that shift in consciousness created by Transmission.

We will explore the role of the Guide in making Transmission possible in the chapter on Guidance.

There are various ways to experience meditation with Transmission: by joining our masterclass series online at heartfulness.org/masterclass, visiting your local Heartfulness Center, calling to request an appointment, requesting a session on the HeartsApp application on your smartphone, requesting a session at www.heartfulness.org, or emailing us at info@heartfulness.org.

Going Deeper

When we are comfortable with the basics of meditation, we start to dive deeper, feeling the Transmission flowing and witnessing what is happening inside. It helps to be alert and conscious, and adjust ourselves to the process.

In the beginning we reach a certain depth and get used to that depth. But after some time, we feel stuck, as if we can't go deeper, as if there is some threshold that can't be crossed. What can we do when this happens? Sometimes we don't feel like meditating; we feel restless and distracted. The trick is to keep going. Soon you will find that the condition changes and you can go deeper again, especially if you have meditation sessions with a trainer capable of imparting Transmission.

Over time, we discover that consciousness has a moving threshold. Can we compare the depth from one year ago to today? When we go beyond a certain threshold, suddenly we are in a new territory or environment. So initially we cannot observe or connect with the new level of consciousness. That is why we lose awareness when we go deep during meditation.

The depth that we feel during meditation as a newcomer and the depth we feel as an adept are different. A small child may have to be held even in one foot of water, but those who know how to swim can survive in an ocean 50 km deep. As we continue to meditate, we gradually get used to different levels of consciousness, because at each step we have journeyed to a new depth. Superficially, it may seem like there is no difference between one state of absorption and another, because we lose awareness each time, but if we look at the condition after meditation, the lightness we felt back then and the lightness we feel today are different. Consciousness is an ever-expanding canvas.

To meditate well, you must have a well-rested mind and heart. Physical rest is a must. A sleepy mind and lethargic body will not take you anywhere. If you are too sleepy to meditate well when you wake up, go for a jog or walk or swim, and then meditate afterward.

To build muscles we may make great plans to go to the gym every day. Some of us go for a couple of days and then lose interest, because it is hard work and the body feels sore. Others are serious, going through vigorous training for three months, six months, or three years, and see the results. It becomes obvious as the muscles strengthen over time. Meditation is also like that, but while the changes we go through because of meditation are invisible changes, we still feel them.

What to Do with Thoughts?

This is a constant problem we all face—the tornado of thoughts arising in our minds all the time. This passage from my first Guide, Babuji, comes from his book *Reality at Dawn,* and gives us some clear guidance on how to work with this problem:

> Generally people complain of numerous ideas creeping into their mind at the time of meditation. They think that they have failed in their practice unless they bring their mind to a standstill. But it is not so. We are not practicing concentration, but only meditation. We must go on with meditation unmindful of the foreign ideas that happen to come to our mind at the time. The flow of ideas is due to the activities of our conscious mind, which is never at rest. We are still busy in meditation with our subconscious mind, while our conscious mind is roaming about and forming numerous ideas. Thus we are not the loser in any way. In due course, after sufficient practice, the conscious mind too gets molded and begins to act in harmony with the subconscious mind. The result thus achieved is deep-rooted and lasting, and finally calmness, the characteristic of the soul, becomes predominant.

There is also a second piece of guidance for managing thoughts. We all want to bring our minds to a still, thoughtless condition during meditation, but what are we doing with our minds the other twenty-three hours of the day? Observe yourself and see. How can it possibly be still for one hour when the rest of the time it is wandering all over the place?

Retain the Meditative State

One way to regulate your mind throughout the day is to remain in a meditative state, carrying the condition you experienced during meditation with you. You can also make the following suggestion wherever you go:

Think that everything around you is absorbed in Godly remembrance. Start by first feeling absorbed in Godly remembrance yourself so its echo will be felt outside.

In this practice, you are allowing the innermost essence of yourself, the Center, to resonate with the innermost essence in everything else—the trees, the birds, the cars, the air particles, etc.—so that everything is absorbed in that essence.

A time will come when you notice that you don't have thoughts at all. The mind is in stillness. Slowly, little by little, it is becoming fine-tuned. This practice of feeling Godly remembrance absorbed even in outer objects keeps your mind focused. It is an amazing benefit, like Yoda says in *Star Wars*: "Luminous beings are we, not this crude matter. You must feel the Force around you. Here, between you, me, the tree, the rock, everywhere. Yes, even between this land and that ship." And there is another benefit: whether you are at the theater or in a shopping mall or college, can you imagine what happens to the feeling around you when you offer this suggestion? Try it as an experiment.

Make this suggestion when you have nothing else to do. You will become absorbed in Godly remembrance, and slowly this absorbency will expand, not just to your immediate surroundings but also to a friend you think of who is living somewhere else. You will send vibrations all over. Allow this feeling to expand. There are no limits to this expansion except those imposed by you. The Earth will be too small; even the Universe will be too small when you allow your consciousness to expand—a consciousness packed with love.

Meditation is also an ever-expanding practice. If you are doing a little today, do a little bit more tomorrow. Try to meditate daily. Then, after you have mastered this, fix your timing to meditate at the same time every day. A time will come when your meditative state will have an echo in others; you will create an impact on them.

Once you can regulate your mind during meditation, the next step is to regulate your mind the rest of the time. Thoughts are rising all the time, but during meditation you become fully aware of what is happening inside, and that is why they speak so loudly.

When you have a session with a trainer, sometimes thoughts arise even more intensely than at other times. When they are good thoughts, you often enjoy them and they seem to expand further and further. But when the thoughts are not so good, when difficult thoughts surface, you may wonder why such thoughts are coming now, and struggle inside. It helps to remember that all these thoughts, good or bad, are only rising from your subconscious to be removed. Very rarely will you be able to recollect the actual thoughts afterward, because they come from the unknown and they go to the unknown. So let them go. Just gently remind yourself that you are meditating.

How do such thoughts get into our subconscious minds in the first place, and how do they make the subconscious their home?

This will be easier to understand when we explore the accumulation of impressions and their cleaning in the next chapter.

Observation

I have always found it very useful to spend a few minutes scanning my system after meditation, to observe how I feel and what has happened inside. Then I write these observations in a journal. I notice different things happening all the time, and sometimes nothing seems to be happening. That is also okay. For example, I may write, "Experienced nothing today," or "My mind was too busy with thoughts to meditate properly." Simply write whatever happens, as a scientist would, and you will also start to notice cycles in your interest in the practice, in your ability to observe within, in your sensitivity to describe different states, and in your moods. You will notice different types of experiences.

Here is a personal example. I was very surprised by an entry I made quite a few years back. At that time, a particular experience seemed very trivial to me. I had written that I saw a particular person during my meditation and we became one. Yesterday, by accident, I opened my diary to that page. It hit me like a rocket. I started crying afterward. It made such an impact, but at the time I wrote it, it meant nothing.

Here is another one. In 1979, when I was still living in India, I had a dream, and in my journal I wrote a description of the place I saw in the dream. It had a stream, giant trees of one hundred and fifty feet, a big canopy, a large lawn, and a small house. In the dream I was seated beside my second Guide, Chariji, and there were four or five others with us. I was even marveling in the dream, "This is a foreign land, and I am in India." Later, in 1986, we were in Atlanta, and Chariji said,

"Let's go to Albany." So five or six of us went to Albany in New York State, and the place we visited was the place I had seen in my dream and described in my journal. I had dreamed about the exact location.

So even if something seems mundane, write it in your journal, for example, "I saw a squirrel." Maybe you will interact with her later on! Write down what you feel in meditation, and you can also write your dreams, the thoughts you have, the feelings you have toward yourself, toward family members, toward others, toward your Guide, toward God, the books that you read, the movies that you see . . . there are so many things.

Now, how do we observe and "read" these inner states, which are also known as conditions? The first step is to create a condition and then let it speak to us. Writing our experiences in a journal cultivates this ability, which is also the first step in retaining that condition.

Reading the inner condition is a relative thing. Imagine trying to read a foreign language that you don't know: for example, Chinese, Tamil, and Greek all look like Martian to me, as I am not used to the letters. At times I do not even know which language is written on paper, but it is enough to know that there is something written. So begin like that. Start with, "Something is written." Then start identifying the letters, then the words, then the sentences, and the subtle nuances. They come automatically when you begin somewhere.

To help with this, before meditating, scan your entire system from top to bottom and observe. Then, slowly, go into meditation. At the end, see if there is any difference between your condition before the meditation and afterward. Then hold on to that difference in your mind.

You may not be able to give a name to it—like the state of Nirvana or the state of detachment or the state of *sat-chit-anand*—but during the day, recall the way it felt. And if it is impressive, then even after one week you will remember, "Last Friday's meditation was special; it was so beautiful." So first get used to the experiences and observe them. What happens later on? It is like giving somebody a mango when he doesn't know its name. Knowing the name is important only when he wants to ask for it to eat it again. But he will say, "I remember that fruit. It was so nice," even if he has forgotten the name. When you have experiences, recollect and recapture them now and then.

There are certain experiences of previous meditation sessions I am unable to forget even today, because they were so impressive and mesmerizing. Was the meditation so important? No, it was the condition that changed me, that lifted me, that still haunts me. When you witness the difference in your state of mind and heart after such a meditation, then you will be able to hold on to it. It doesn't matter what you call it.

Create a Meditative State

In every meditation there is something unique that is bestowed upon us. This is how we receive spiritual nourishment or earn spiritual wealth. How do we then preserve the new condition that has been gifted to us?

The first step is to become sensitive enough to know that we are being given spiritual nourishment, and then to make efforts to retain it, preserve it, and let it grow. I call it: **a**cquire, **e**nliven, **i**mbibe, become **o**ne with it, and eventually reach a state of **u**nion, or AEIOU. We secure it so that it becomes one with us. We merge with it. AEIOU is easy to remember.

It requires only five minutes after meditation to observe ourselves within, to try to recognize and become one with our condition, savor it, enliven it, and make it ours. Then it has a chance to grow. When we sharpen a knife, we do so to cut vegetables. When we sharpen our consciousness, it is to be used during the daytime. It helps to know how sharp our consciousness is. During morning Meditation, we achieve a certain level of consciousness. When we hold on to it and carry on with our day-to-day activities, we retain a full grip over the morning condition with open eyes.

What does "grip over the condition" mean? Here is an analogy: suppose someone tells you a joke, and later on at home you remember the joke and it makes you laugh aloud. Your son asks, "Daddy, what's up?" So you explain, "I remembered a joke." In the same way, the condition arising out of morning Meditation may be so good, so profound, and so intense that it comes back to you. You learn to walk with it, work with it, relax with it, and imbibe it fully. That is the meditative state we try to carry with us day and night.

Once serenity and purity are created within through meditation, we learn how to hold on to them. This is the art known as "meditation with open eyes" or "constant remembrance," in which we carry the condition received during meditation throughout the day into all aspects of our life.

To achieve this, those five or six minutes after meditation are so productive. Use them wisely to your advantage. The inner meditative condition is subtler than the fragrance of a rose. It can easily dissipate into thin air so that we cannot recall it. So there are a few things to avoid immediately after meditation in order to retain the condition that has been given to us:

Try not to draw your attention outward straight after meditation. This means not changing things in the outer environment. If the fan is on, let it be on. If the fan is not on, don't turn it on, because it will draw your attention outward. Similarly, avoid drinking water immediately after meditation. When someone is crying or you have to give bad news to someone, you go with a glass of water so that the person quiets down, because it redirects their attention from inward to outward. In that situation, by giving water you are changing the condition for the better. After we meditate, the condition can be lost by drinking water for the same reason—it redirects our attention outward.

Take the example of freshly laid concrete; it is better not to walk on it until it has settled properly. If we walk on it, allow dogs to run over it, and let someone write, "I love Monica" on it, then that concrete is spoiled forever. Like concrete, our inner condition also has to settle in our heart, and it needs attention. Observe how it settles inside you, feel how it drenches your system, and then, when you are confident that you can observe and hold on to it even with your open eyes, confidently get up and carry on with your day.

The condition you receive in meditation is much finer and subtler than concrete. Mere carelessness can make it disappear. So be tender and careful with it. Spend five minutes to savor it, absorb it, and then get up with the resolution that you are getting all the help you need to nurture it and let it grow. The guidance will come from inside you. Have the willingness, interest, and intention to preserve it and let it grow.

Try to remain in that meditative state with your open eyes. Center yourself in your heart, be perceptive, and try to understand things with your heart. When you observe things around you, keep your attention in the heart. Let your inner radar open up. If you want to become very discerning, this is the habit to cultivate!

A mind that is not balanced loses its radar, its direction. A pure mind finds its direction within because it is centered. A settled mind finds its own center. So, meditation ultimately brings you to your center and makes it palpable. You then have inner guidance all the time, and it speaks to you, especially about wrong things. About truth it may not speak at all, because truth is its nature.

The very first step or attainment in spirituality is discernment. Without the ability to discriminate between right and wrong, good and bad, honorable and disreputable, your inner radar is lost. When you have a pure heart, that inner radar is very powerful. With a pure heart, you can know so many things.

As the meditative state deepens into constant remembrance, the whole spectrum of consciousness remains in contact with your Center, as the substratum of your existence, and over time this underlying connection blossoms into love. Just as we always remember those we love, the reverse also holds true: the more we remember, the more love develops.

If you have to define Heartfulness, it is love. It is a love story between our "self" and our Creator. In the beginning we do not know what the Creator or God is, and it is difficult to fall in love with something we don't know. So we start with our focus on our side of the relationship, on "I," looking inward. Then the Guide comes to our aid. The Guide is experienced and comfortable in this realm of God, so he gently shifts our attention away from "I" toward "we." This "I" and "we" dynamic evolves and expands over time through many levels of consciousness. He is also someone with whom we can identify on the human level as we go through these levels of consciousness. The more he helps us, through his Transmission and his support, the more we appropriate his help and the more gratitude we feel toward him, as our attention moves from the gifts to the giver. This gratitude leads us to remember him more often, and after some time love also dawns. At some point we feel so much love, and we don't know how it has happened.

This all starts with the simple act of meditation. Meditation is the mother of constant remembrance. Without a mother there is no child; without mother-meditation there is no constant remembrance.

This ability to remain in the meditative state all throughout the day while still doing other things is another process that we all understand very well—it is not something difficult. Think about a child learning to ride a bicycle. When you first teach your child, you bring home a tricycle and help her by holding on to it while she learns to pedal it properly. From a tricycle, you then bring her a two-wheeler bicycle with two trainer wheels at the back. After some practice, you remove the trainer wheels and she is on two wheels. Then what happens? She goes to kindergarten or to school on a bigger bicycle. She rides with her friends, chatting away, singing, and watching the traffic, remembering where she is going. She observes things while still riding her bicycle. It is easy for a child and does not take long.

If a child can master the art of cycling while doing other things, we can also master the art of pedaling the spiritual condition. Of course we will forget now and then, but if we are really interested, then we will start pedaling each condition after meditation, and we will learn how to do other things while maintaining the meditative state. If we learn how to pedal our condition during the daytime, we can be doing so many things at the same time. That is constant remembrance—it is simple.

Be Like a Lotus

In certain environments it is more difficult to maintain that inner condition. For example, students complain about this in their college accommodation, but anything can be detrimental if you allow it to be. I also lived in a hostel from the ninth grade until I did my master's degree, and I learned that you can turn the adverse situation to your advantage.

If some of your friends make fun of you for meditating, challenge them by saying, "Look, I assure you this will do you a lot of good." Ask your friends, "Do you want to change? This will help you to change." When I was at college, one of my friends couldn't sleep, and when he did sleep it was at the wrong time. So we enticed him, "Come and meditate, and your sleep pattern will improve." In the very first meditation session his sleep pattern was normalized. Another fellow did not know how to study well. His focus was so poor that our professors said, "Go with Kamlesh. He will take you for meditation. It will improve." At one time we had more than twenty-five students meditating, so a trainer would give us meditation sessions in our hostel. It really depends on what we make of any situation. Simplicity is not a weakness. Purity is not a weakness. They are mighty if we allow them to be.

As we nurture the subtle conditions bestowed during meditation, over time they create a beautiful environment. Imagine what sort of environment can be created at home when we meditate; our family members meditate, and our friends also come home and meditate. There will be so much lightness, peace, and joy. Everyone will feel happy in that space.

An atmosphere that is created by our collective thoughts and feelings is called an *egregore*. When we all meditate together, we create a subtle field of loving unity. And when enough people meditate, a particular tipping point in the egregore will be reached. Then the course of humanity will change.

CHAPTER 4

LETTING GO OF THE PAST: CLEANING

ONE OF THE problems we all face while meditating is the distraction caused by our own thoughts and feelings. We need something to clear our field of consciousness, creating stillness in the mind. In Heartfulness we have a practice of mental detoxification called Cleaning. It helps us to dive deeper into meditation, removing the impurities, complexities, and emotional heaviness that accumulate during the day in our minds. We feel lighter and more carefree. These complexities and impurities accumulate as a result of repeated patterns of feeling, emotion, and thought, which, in turn, lead to repetitive actions. These actions become habits that impress upon our minds, creating fixed patterns of behavior that become more and more fixed over time, forming impressions in our subtle body.

As the English proverb says:

Sow a thought and reap an action,
Sow an action and reap a habit,
Sow a habit and reap a character,
Sow a character and reap a destiny.

How Do We Form Impressions?

Imagine for a minute that you are walking in a garden and you notice the exquisite fragrance of a rose in the air. The next day when you walk past the same place, you become more aware of the beautiful fragrance, and you look for the rose bush. You find it, go closer, and observe how beautiful it is. After enjoying both the fragrance and its visual beauty, you walk on. On the third day you hold the flower, and on the fourth day you pluck it and take it home. That is how we form impressions. We are not happy with one inhalation of fragrance. We want to own it, we want to possess it, and then we are caught!

There is a story about a saint who was peacefully meditating in a jungle. He had no problems. He was blissful and well respected by the villagers nearby. He had only a loincloth to worry about, which he would wash and hang on a tree branch at night. But some little mice started eating it while it hung on the branch, and his loincloth was slowly becoming smaller and smaller.

So the villagers suggested, "Let's get you a cat."

They got him a cat to chase away the mice, but to keep a cat you have to give it milk all the time. So somebody started bringing milk every evening to feed the cat until they got tired of it.

They said, "How can we come every evening and risk our lives returning back to the village?"

So they decided to get him a cow. Now somebody needed to milk the cow that fed the cat that caught the mice that ate the loincloth. They sent a maid to milk the cow. He fell in love with that maid and started a family. One little desire triggered this chain reaction!

It doesn't matter if a wish is fulfilled or not or whether it is attainable or not; as long as it is a seed in your mind, it will wait for an opportunity to germinate. It may stay buried for ten lifetimes. As a small boy, you may have really wanted a certain little remote-controlled car, and now as an adult that impression still haunts you: "I have to buy that sort of car!" Until you get it, you are miserable. And the biggest problem is that generally we are not even conscious of such wishes.

Swami Vivekananda describes this process of formation of impressions and the resulting cognates we develop in his book, *Jnana Yoga*: "Suppose I go into the street and see a dog. How do I know it is a dog? I refer it to my mind, and in my mind are groups of all my past experiences, arranged and pigeon-holed, as it were. As soon as a new impression comes, I take it up and refer it to some of the old pigeon-holes, and as soon as I find a group of the same impressions already existing, I place it in that group, and I am satisfied. I know it is a dog, because it coincides with the impressions already there.

"When I do not find the cognates of this new experience inside, I become dissatisfied. When, not finding the cognates of an impression, we become dissatisfied, this state of the mind is called 'ignorance'; but, when, finding the cognates of an impression already existing, we become satisfied, this is called 'knowledge.' When one apple fell, men became dissatisfied. Then gradually they found out the group. What was the group they found? That all apples fall, so they called it 'gravitation.' Now we see that without a fund of already existing experience, any new experience would be impossible, for there would be nothing to which to refer the new impression."[1]

---

1. Swami Vivekananda, "The Cosmos, The Microcosm," *Jnana Yoga* (USA: Vedanta Press, 1899), chapter 12.

Any thought or action can lead to an impression, and when the thoughts or actions repeat themselves, they lead to habits, creating rigid thought patterns, which become more and more solid over time.

Imagine that your mind is completely pure and still, like a crystal-clear pool of water in utter stillness, in which you can see all the way to the bottom. Now, a thought, an emotion, or an experience enters that field, and creates ripples and turbulence, just as a disturbance does in water. If that disturbance is not removed, it creates a knot of energy, an impression. As the impression deepens and hardens, it becomes fixed into a samskara. Samskaras are the base of our habits, our fears, and our desires, which then are repeated over and over again, just as a trickle of water forms a stream then eventually a river as water follows the same path.

Unless we remove samskaras, we stay trapped in our patterns and we cannot break free, no matter how much we may want to change.

We are not able to change the past, but we can remove the samskaras that have formed as a result of our past. If today's existence is about working off these older samskaras, how is tomorrow's existence formed? We can clean all our previous samskaras in this life, but are we going to continue to form more? This topic is one of the most important aspects of how we design our future destiny.

There is also another way we form impressions, and that is by watching TV, movies, and video games. We become affected when we watch a violent scene or a romantic scene. The drama may not be from our own lives, but after watching the program we absorb those impressions, and before going to sleep the same reel goes on in our minds. What happens to our heart at that time? Does it remain placid and unaffected? Often it is affected just as it would be in real life. Can we remain immune to such impressions?

There is no need to stop watching TV or movies, but we do need to sensitize ourselves to forming such impressions and, whenever possible, vaccinate ourselves against them. The only vaccination I know is to remain absorbed in the deepest level of our consciousness by connecting with our highest Self within. Then we remain like a lotus in the water, unaffected by the mud all around us. Otherwise we remain vulnerable.

There is another aspect to this modern pastime of TV and the Internet. What are they all about? They remind us of our incompleteness. They remind us that, "Your husband is not like this," or "Your children should be like this." They remind us that we do not have a house like this, we want a car like this, we do not have friends like this, we should eat food like this, and we must visit this or that holiday destination. We sit there filling our minds with expectations and dreams, with fantasies, fairy tales, and excitement that are not in our own lives. We will always feel that dissatisfied sense of "If only my life was like that!"

Types of Impressions

What types of impressions dominate our lives? There can be so many types, for example, worldly worries, sexual attraction to other people and problems in relationships, prejudices, greed, grief, sadness, self-pity, guilt, and shame. But as well as impressions formed by our thoughts and actions, we also form impressions by our inactions, creating more guilt. These are the things that we should do but don't do, and such things haunt us all our lives. For example, we may have hurt someone very dear to us without ever having said sorry. Impressions like that are difficult to remove.

Also, as well as forming our own impressions, what about those times when we become the instrument of forming impressions in the lives of others? For example, a simple throw-away criticism can hurt another person so deeply that they are disturbed for days. A flirtatious glance from a pretty girl can leave a young man gaga for weeks. And if we go on polluting this beautiful planet with our careless lifestyles, definitely there will be a consequence to our actions.

Another way to look at all of this is that the formation of samskaras happens when we deviate from the principle of leading a life with love. We become unnatural, and such an unnatural life means that we form samskaras.

There is a funny story about this: Once upon a time, a Japanese master welcomed a university professor who came to inquire about Zen. The master served tea, and when he poured the tea into the professor's cup, he kept on pouring after it had overflowed.

The professor watched this for some time, until he could no longer keep quiet: "It is overflowing. Please stop."

"Like this cup, you are full of your own opinions and beliefs," said the Zen master. "How can I teach you unless you first empty your cup?"

Heartfulness Cleaning

We do the practice of Heartfulness Cleaning at the end of the working day, ideally before sunset, refreshing ourselves and creating a vacuum within, purifying our system of its accumulated heaviness. Although it is simple, there are a number of steps to Cleaning, so in the beginning it is better to practice them in sequence, as follows:

- Sit in a comfortable position with the intention to remove all the impressions accumulated during the day.

- Close your eyes and feel relaxed.

- Imagine all the complexities and impurities are leaving your entire system.

- They are going out from your back, from the top of your head to your tailbone.

- Feel they are leaving your system as smoke.

- Remain alert during the entire process, like a witness to the clouds passing in the sky.

- Gently accelerate this process with confidence and determination, applying your will as needed.

- If your attention drifts and events of the day begin to come to mind, gently bring your focus back to the cleaning.

- As the impressions are leaving from your back, you will start to feel light in your heart.

- Continue this process for 20 to 25 minutes.

- When you experience inner lightness, you will naturally find it easy to connect with the Source.

> Feel a current of purity coming from the Source and entering your system from the front.
>
> - This current is flowing throughout your system, carrying away any remaining complexities and impurities.
>
> - You have now returned to a simpler, purer, and more balanced state. Every cell of your body is emanating simplicity, lightness, and purity.

After some practice, just like pedaling a bicycle, you will no longer need to suggest all of these individual steps to yourself. The moment you close your eyes, they will start happening on their own and you will not need words.

But even when you do the Cleaning regularly, as prescribed, you may still wonder, "Have I done it correctly?" How can you judge that you have completed the Cleaning the way it should be done? Here is one way: do a comparative study when you go to a trainer. After a meditation session with a trainer, study your condition and see how it is. Do you have a similar lightness after you do your own Cleaning at home? If the answer is yes, then you have done a good job with the Cleaning process. Otherwise, keep going.

What Is Being Cleaned

When we clean in the evening, we unload the impressions that we collect during the day and create a vacuum in the heart. The practice of Cleaning removes the impressions that accumulate in our subtle body, in the same way that we take a bath to clean away the dirt from the physical body.

What is being purified? It is our consciousness, and this then has a ripple effect on our whole worldview, bringing clarity, understanding, and wisdom. A pure consciousness is able to easily discern and make wise choices. In fact, Lalaji once said, "The soul of a human being will be clean in proportion to the power of discrimination they possess." The purer the heart, the more wisdom we will have. When this protective wisdom is gone, we become vulnerable. This is very practical guidance for anyone who wishes to live a life full of wisdom. It also highlights the importance of the Cleaning practice.

When to Do Cleaning

Generally we practice Cleaning at the end of the day, but what if something happens during the day that affects us despite our best efforts to remain calm? Do we wait until evening to remove the effect on our system? When your hands get dirty during the day, do you wait until the evening bath to wash them? If you accidentally spill food on your shirt while having lunch, do you leave the stain there till evening? No. You spot clean your shirt with water and soap immediately to minimize the staining.

Similarly, if you have an argument, or something happens that disturbs you, remove it then and there. Make a subtle suggestion: "What has affected me right now is going from the back in the form of smoke." After a few minutes, when you are confident that the impression has gone, make a firm resolution that it has really gone. Perhaps it is not possible to close your eyes, because you are in class or in a meeting, but you can still clean for a few minutes.

So Cleaning changes everything! As samskaras are removed, the past loses its hold over us. The trajectory of our karmic destiny is no longer fixed, and we have the opportunity to mold our lives into what they ought to be.

How to Avoid Forming Impressions

Cleaning removes the impressions that have already formed in our system, but how do we stop them from forming in the first place? Some simple attitudes and behaviors will help. For example, if you are having an argument, and you know it is not leading anywhere and will disturb your consciousness for the rest of the day, then stop arguing and simply say, "I am sorry." Take a step back during the process and pause. You have a choice. Prevention is a wise option.

Imagine you have a bad day at the office and come home with a lot of tension and frustration. Your poor wife has also had a hectic day and is trying to cook dinner for the kids, who are tired and hungry. What happens? Do you pamper each other? Very often, in such circumstances, you argue. So, instead, when you know your day has been stressful, first cool down. As soon as you enter the house, wash your face and sit for Cleaning. Afterward you will have a fresh consciousness, a renewed consciousness, and then you will not trigger any conflict with your family or friends. You can say that your consciousness is protective, as you won't argue and you will prevent a lot of impressions from gathering and spoiling your consciousness.

Such a lifestyle is so much better than reacting to every little thing. But this is also not the ultimate, ideal lifestyle, because it is still defensive. The ideal life is carefree, because we *do not form impressions.* That is self-mastery, the life of a Master or Guide. Instead of forming impressions, they help others to stop forming impressions. We are aiming at such a lifestyle where nothing touches us. How is that possible when we have to live in the world? Remember the meditative state? Our consciousness is a twenty-four-hour business. By evolving and expanding our consciousness, after some time we do not even think of it as protective, because it is our existence itself. It is not something we have to invoke, because we *are* that.

The more we retain the meditative state after morning Meditation, the easier it is to live a life in which we don't form impressions. And we already know the method to do this: meditating with eyes open. In this state we are drowned in love, resting in absolute osmosis with the Guide, and going about all our other activities in this state. This demands a conscious lifestyle.

Emotional Reactions

We can remove impressions by Heartfulness Cleaning, but what about all the behavioral patterns and habits that define us as individuals? Do they also disappear automatically when we clean the impressions, or do we need to do something more about them?

Those patterns often lead to emotional reactions and traits that are habitual. Take the story of Mulla Nasruddin, who complained every day at lunchtime that he was tired of having the same salad sandwiches for lunch. His colleagues listened to these complaints over and over for a few weeks and then suggested a solution.

"Dear Mulla, how about telling your wife to make something different? Encourage her to be more creative."

"Oh, I am not married," replied the Mulla.

"Then who makes your lunch for you?"

"I do," replied the Mulla.

What are our "salad sandwich" patterns? And what are we doing to change them?

We can liken impressions and behavioral tendencies to water flowing in a river. Imagine that samskaras are like the water in the river; the water can be removed, just as we remove the samskaras, but what happens when it rains again? If the riverbed is there, the water will start flowing again in the same old pattern. The riverbed is the field of our habits, so we re-create the same samskaras because we do not let go of the behavioral patterns. The only solution is to remove the riverbed.

How do we do that? Personally I have learned to cultivate a carefree attitude, which leads to a state of acceptance. Not only is it possible, it is easier than you might imagine. The simple formula is: meditate, retain, and grow. One step takes you to the next. Take one step at a time. Practice first, and everything else will follow. Sometimes it is difficult, because we do not know what will follow. It is like driving on a foggy road at night in the mountains when you can't see anything. You drive slowly, and the way becomes clearer as you continue. If you stop driving, you won't reach anywhere. The spiritual journey is also like that. We need to walk with faith in our own abilities, our own belief, and our own trust and confidence. Invoke that. When we do our part well, the Guide is able to do his so much better.

Think of the most beautiful music. Now imagine if the instruments playing it were not kept clean. Would that beautiful sound emerge? Imagine a flute so clogged up with dust and saliva that the sound emerging from it is distorted. Imagine a guitar with rusty strings. The heart, like the flute and the guitar, produces beautiful music when it is not so caught up with the complexities of life. As we become simpler and purer with Cleaning, the heart becomes ready to receive the ultimate bounties. In such a heart, heaven descends.

CHAPTER 5

CONNECTING WITH THE
SOURCE: PRAYER

SO FAR WE have explored Relaxation, Meditation, and Cleaning. The next Heartfulness practice is Prayer. Most people associate prayer with religion, as a way to entreat God: a plea, an earnest hope, or wish for something more than we are or have, for something to fill us. It is designed to take us from our current state to our desired state.

We pray for things we feel are lacking. Often we pray in times of difficulty, and we pray for help, for hope, and for salvation. We pray for the well-being of our loved ones, we pray to be forgiven for things we have done, we pray to change our character and attitudes, and we pray for happiness, more money, a better job, or healthy children. We hope that God will fix our suffering and our problems so that our lives and the lives of others become better. Often we do this when we are at our wits' end, when we cannot solve the problems on our own, and when we see our own weaknesses mirrored in the world around us.

At a deeper level, we pray for spiritual states that we feel are lacking so that we can grow and evolve. We may pray for enlightenment, nirvana, heaven, liberation, and God-realization. Prayer can be selfish or selfless, it can be forceful or subtle, it can be for little things or life-changing events, and it can be for worldly things or spiritual states.

Prayer is communication. It can range from the superficial to the profound: it can be a simple conversation, it can evolve to progressively deeper levels of communication, and eventually, it can become a state of communion. Prayer thus evolves as a potent way to communicate with God. Prayer is about connection and how we activate the flow of Transmission through that connection. Prayer is also about how we eventually establish a state of osmosis in that flow.

The concept is similar to the way fluids create differentials across cell walls in plants and animals so that nutrients can flow into the cells for nourishment. In prayer we create a similar differential between the Divine and ourselves to allow Divinity to flow into us and nourish us on a spiritual level. It is simple science. We create that differential by cultivating a state of vacuum in our heart so that the current of Divinity flows in, eventually leading to a state of osmosis with the Divine. That state of vacuity or negation also establishes a relationship of devotion with the Divine. And this is what allows us to attain the state of highest purity.

How to Pray

When we pray, both the manner and the matter are important. The manner is the way we pray. What is our attitude at the time? How do we create a condition within us so that the current of Divinity flows into our heart?

The process is so simple, so beautiful, and so scientific. The attitudes of humility, supplicancy, innocence, and insignificance create a vacuum in the heart so that the current from the Source flows in and enlivens the connection, just as electrical current flows from the positive to the negative pole in an electrical wire. Our job is to create the negative polarity by allowing a receptive, yielding state within the heart.

If we are not yielding, if our attitude is strong or demanding, with self-importance or force, then no vacuum is created in the heart, so there is no flow. It is a natural phenomenon, and our manner creates the condition for the flow to be activated or not. The subtlety in the way we offer prayer makes a huge difference to this flow. How gentle and yielding is our request? How light is our touch? Also, the moment prayer becomes a ritual it loses its potency.

I was once with Chariji in his bedroom while we were traveling, and at one point he woke up, sat on the bed, and closed his eyes. After a few moments the whole atmosphere in the room changed. It was so palpable. After he had finished, I asked him what he had been doing, and he replied, "Praying to Babuji." Prayer can be such a potent practice, and it's largely underutilized by most of us.

In a way, prayer is an inner cry where pearls of tears slowly flow down our face and beautify the inner complexities of the heart. A prayerful heart carries the eternal fragrance or essence of Divinity wherever it goes. It is an expression of love that can only be shared with the Beloved. A heart drowned in prayer keeps us alert to our goal, and this absorbency also helps us to recognize our defects and find possible solutions to remove them.

Then there is the matter, the subject of our prayers. We pray for many different things. One type of prayer is for the removal of unwanted behaviors, worries, concerns, or situations that bring us suffering. Such prayers are usually a cry for help. They are often to alleviate the sufferings of others. They can also be for our own suffering, especially when the situation is dire and no help is coming in other ways. This is the last resort of a karma yogi. When such a prayer is a cry of feeling from one's heart, it is easily heard.

The second type of prayer is a very positive cry for continuous improvement, to acquire noble qualities, to grow and evolve. The following are some examples of such prayerful suggestion that I like very much.

The Practice of Prayerful Suggestion

All humanity is developing correct thinking,
right understanding, and an honest approach to life.
They are attaining rightness in action and
perfection in character.

Everything surrounding us—people,
the air particles, the birds, the trees—is
deeply absorbed in Godly remembrance.

All people of the world are growing peace-loving.

Then there are prayers where we don't need anything to change. Instead we offer prayers filled with gratitude, accepting whatever is happening in the moment. Take, for example, when the heart is ecstatic and joyful, and we are able to share our joy with God, just as we share our sorrow with an inner cry. When the heart rejoices in this state of reverence and gratitude, it connects us with Divinity. In all societies, this inner joy is expressed prayerfully through dance, devotional songs, art, etc.

But even our gratitude is in response to a particular state, in this case the feeling of joy and ecstasy. There is still an expectation that we are grateful for something wonderful that has happened.

The Heartfulness Prayer operates at a different level altogether—one where we do not entreat any change. Instead, we offer three simple statements that define our human condition. The words remind us of our spiritual goal, the obstacles we face on the journey, and what helps us to reach there. There is no stated expectation in this Prayer, but there is still the feeling of differential, that we are not yet "up to that stage," that there is an infinite journey ahead of us, and that we must continually refine and remove our wishes if there is a hope to experience finer and finer states. While offering this Prayer, we honor the present moment in our journey as well as acknowledging that the journey must continue.

The Heartfulness Prayer is done at bedtime for ten to fifteen minutes, to help us connect with our Source before sleep. It is also done for a few minutes before meditating in the morning as a way of resetting that connection. By beginning and ending the day this way, a connection is established with the Source throughout the day and night. And, over time, self-mastery develops through this inner connection.

Heartfulness Prayer

Sit in a comfortable position, gently close your eyes, and relax. With a feeling of humility and love, silently and slowly let these words resonate within the space in your heart. You can repeat them a couple of times, pausing in between.

O Master!
Thou art the real goal of human life.
We are yet but slaves of wishes
putting bar to our advancement.
Thou art the only God and Power
to bring us up to that stage.

Meditate for ten to fifteen minutes over the true sense of the words and try to get lost in them.

Let the feeling behind the words come to you.

Allow yourself to melt into this prayerful feeling.

The words are a springboard—they are supposed to remind us of the feeling behind them. Eventually there will be no words at all, and a total acceptance of whatever the present moment gives, and this brings about the most profound state of prayerfulness.

The Heartfulness Prayer leads us toward the ultimate state of osmosis, of homeostasis, or total mergence with the Lord, but it is asymptotic. It never actually arrives. The differential we experience through prayer between God and ourselves will always be necessary, as only with that differential do we keep swimming onward, with the current flowing through our heart, connecting us to our Center.

What Is the Result of Prayer?

Two vital things come together in the act of prayer, and when they combine they can create the potential for lasting change and real growth. This is one of Nature's open secrets.

On the one hand, prayer connects you with your highest Self through the heart, to dive so deep that you connect with the Source of everything. On the other hand, it uses the power of thought or suggestion to bring about change, and this we call *sankalpa* in Yoga.

Sankalpa works better than orders or instructions, because it is so potent. The English translation for sankalpa is usually "suggestion," although it is not an adequate translation. A suggestion is a type of thought—one in which an idea is put forward for change, usually with some idea of improvement or vision. So a prayerful suggestion is a very subtle suggestion that resonates in a pure, open, loving heart connected to the Divine. As an aside, have you ever thought about the fact that negative suggestion is the cause of most of the failures of humanity? This is true even with the suggestions we make to ourselves, about ourselves, through auto-suggestion.

The way we use suggestion in prayer is most important. There is no need to say please, because even the word *please* is too heavy. And the offering of "May such and such a thing happen," while slightly gentler, is also not subtle enough. How can we pray so that we do not disturb the divine silence? That is the ideal prayer.

These two processes of connecting and sankalpa combine like elements in a chemical reaction to create a dynamic state of communion with our inner essence. In prayer we are deep within the heart, so the thought or feeling we offer to the Lord is not just a thought, a theoretical, or an intellectual thing. It resonates across the canvas of our consciousness through the heart into the cosmic field, or quantum field if you like. The effect is so potent. It is no longer from our own individual level. It becomes a key to unlock evolution, to bring about transformation.

In the Heartfulness Prayer we commune with our highest Self, our inner Divinity. In the process we develop self-mastery by acknowledging the rightful place of this higher Self at the center of our lives. But it is not only an acknowledgment. We actually refer to that higher Self when we are prayerful, and so gradually we master the art of listening to the heart.

The words of the prayer are supposed to invoke feeling in us. Once feeling is there, we no longer need the words. A time comes when the prayerful state is always there, when the few seconds we take to offer prayer at night expand into twenty-four hours, when our inner Master is always in focus, and we are always in tune with ourselves, prayerfully maintaining the condition we have.

We are prayerful, we are maintaining the condition, and we are allowing it to grow. So no matter what we are doing—studying, watching television, taking a shower, eating breakfast, with friends, partying—the inner connection is always there.

That is the beauty of Heartfulness. It doesn't take away any of our time. When we master the practice, it requires less and less time, and yet it remains a twenty-four-hour business.

So start with the words. Each word of this bedtime prayer can unlock some sort of feeling in your heart. Follow that feeling, contemplate on that feeling, and sleep in that mood. It will transform your life.

CHAPTER 6

ATTITUDE

IMAGINE THAT NOW you are doing these four Heartfulness practices every day: Relaxation, Meditation, Cleaning, and Prayer. Even for the best of us, doing any set of practices day after day can become a repetitive process, whether it is swimming, athletics, playing a musical instrument, calligraphy, cardiac surgery, or meditation. The mechanics are always repetitive. So what makes an endeavor come alive and develop vibrancy? It is attitude and interest. Attitude is 95 percent of success. I have found that the attitudes of love, humility, and prayerfulness have helped me a lot.

Think of it like this: you ask a girl out on a first date to the cinema, and you are so keen to meet her that you arrive an hour beforehand, or even earlier. You anticipate her arrival with so much inner excitement. But then what happens if you are waiting and she doesn't show up until five minutes before the movie begins? It feels like eternity, and you are so restless. Do you have the same sort of impatience, enthusiasm, and passion for meditation? Do you feel so inspired to meet your inner Self during meditation? That attitude brings life to meditation.

Before you go to sleep, anticipate your meditation in the morning. Suggest to your higher Self, "I am eagerly looking forward to meeting you tomorrow morning." Practice with such interest that you become cognizant of everything that passes through you, both the transmission and the samskaras. The samskaras were yours before they went out, so feel the difference when they are gone. It helps so much to create fascination, passion, and restlessness toward the practice itself. Otherwise it is only labor, dry and mechanical, and then it is not worthwhile.

Imagine a laborer on the farm, earning his daily wage doing a lot of hard physical work, but complaining about his work constantly. He may work the whole day, but he does not build the same muscle mass as another man who goes to the gym, only spending half an hour a day working out. It is all a matter of attitude. If your practice is purely mechanical, if you think, "Oh no! I have to wake up and meditate," or if you do it only to satisfy someone else, there is no need to do it at all, because you will waste your time.

With anything that you do, make sure you do it joyfully and cheerfully. And if you really enjoy meditation, you can do it again and again throughout the day. Of course you don't need to stop doing other things, but there is no need to limit yourself to once every morning.

A Daily Routine

Over the years I've learned another very important attitude from my Guides, which has helped me to deepen my meditation practice and bring it alive: automatism. What do I mean by this? There are two aspects to automatism. The first is that I learned to recall the meditative state at any given moment, even with my eyes open, and the second is that I fixed my timings so as to establish a biological clock in my practice.

What is this biological clock? You have probably heard about the classic behavioral experiments carried out by the Russian scientist Dr. Ivan Pavlov in the 1890s. He performed experiments in which he rang a bell and served food to dogs at the same time every day. He conditioned the dogs for some time, then one day he rang the bell and gave no food so the dogs went crazy, barking and salivating profusely. That is a learned associated response.

We also develop a learned associated response by meditating at the same time every day, and after some time as soon as we sit to meditate we easily go into meditation because we are attuned to it. It is as simple as starting with a resolution to fix your timing for meditation and sticking to it. It may be six o'clock, seven o'clock, or whatever time works for you. The main thing is to be consistent. It is more important to be consistent than to meditate one day at eight, one day at nine, one day at six, and one day at three in the morning, for two hours or one hour. Then, after some time, you will one day realize that you feel the same way as the salivating dogs the day you are not able to meditate at your regular hour. Do you miss it? That is the key.

When your meditations are predictable, others also respect your routine and give you space. Once your friends and family know you meditate at six o'clock, they will not disturb you at that time. But if you keep meditating randomly, no one knows when you meditate and then they will disturb you.

I grew up in a village in Gujarat in India. In the morning after sunrise, the buffaloes were let free into the village and the farms for grazing. In the evening they all came back together, entering the village, and each one found its own street, and in that street its own *khoont,* the stump to which it was tied up at night. It didn't go anywhere else, even by mistake. It didn't make mistakes. It went to the right house, the right stump, and was tied there for the night.

We can also fix our place for meditation. We sometimes have the habit of meditating on the sofa one morning, on the bed the next, and on the train when we are running late for work. But it helps to fix our place, because the atmosphere in that place becomes refined over time. Then when we sit it is so much easier to meditate. If we are as wise as the buffaloes, we will find one place.

Love Attracts

Another beautiful thing that I have learned over the years is that love attracts. People who have a hard heart and a harsh face repel grace, whereas a joyful heart attracts grace easily and naturally. When I worked in business, with fifty employees, I came to know the differences between people. There was a spectrum of facial expressions and attitudes in their work. When someone worked joyfully and came on time, I wanted to work with that person, and I was happy to have them in the organization. If a person was always complaining, "I don't like this," "I will not do this," "I cannot come now," it was not so easy to tolerate them, and when they went away, nobody missed them. But a really good worker, a really good employee who mastered the work, was missed even when they were absent for a day. Their absence spoke louder than their presence.

Similarly, in our spiritual practice, we move to another dimension if we are able to bring about regularity, cheerfulness, and restlessness to achieve the best.

Staying in tune with that pedaling all the time, with that spiritual condition we achieve in the morning, is not going to disturb our daily activities. In fact, when we are in higher levels of consciousness, the time we spend working also reduces. Work requires less and less time, and when we need to study we are able to read with a calm, peaceful, and composed mind. We absorb everything in one reading. Others have to read the same passage again and again.

Through Heartfulness practices our actions move toward perfection, although there will always be room for improvement, and we will always be striving to become perfect. The Guide is also striving to achieve perfection, both within as well as in the work, constantly asking, "How much can I change so that my work becomes more effective?" All of us can try our best to become better and better all the time.

Cooperation

One quality that is vital in spiritual practice is cooperation. Imagine for a moment that we are going on a trek to the summit of Mount Everest, or as an astronaut we are journeying into space. We accept the importance of following instructions in those situations. Also, we accept the importance of following a doctor's advice when we have a life-threatening illness. Similarly, on the spiritual journey it is important to follow a Guide who has mastered the journey, because we are traversing the inner universe.

It is not that meditation gives us everything, but meditation done properly creates a condition, and that condition changes us. Once that inner environment is changed, faith develops in a natural way. Once faith develops, acceptance also comes. Once acceptance is established, surrender develops. Then we fall in love with the Giver, and this leads to losing ourselves in a state of oneness with the Giver; it becomes child's play. This is known as mergence in spirituality. So when understood in this way, spiritual growth is only difficult for those of us who cannot cooperate.

The Power of Suggestion

Heartfulness is based on the power of suggestion, which is also known as sankalpa. We have already touched upon this in the earlier section on prayer. But there are different levels of subtlety of suggestion, which are demonstrated in the following example:

Three friends go out to dinner. The restaurant is busy, and they are impatiently waiting to order their food, as they are in a rush.

One of them shouts at the waiter as he is passing by, "Hey, come here! We want to order!"

It is an order. The waiter acknowledges him and says he will be back soon. Five minutes pass and another waiter comes by.

The second friend is more courteous and says, "We would like to order."

It is a request—not as forceful, but still commanding. The second waiter also replies that he will return shortly.

A while later, the waiter returns, and the third friend smiles and suggests, "We are ready whenever you are, thanks."

The waiter smiles back and takes the order.

The last one gives the subtlest suggestion of the three, more like a hint. And what a grand difference there is between these three approaches. Which do you think has the most potent effect? As with everything in nature, the subtlest is always the most effective. A forceful approach is more likely to meet with resistance, just like in Newton's third law of motion: for every action, there is an equal and opposite reaction.

Similarly, you can use different levels of subtlety of thought while doing your practice. For example, while doing the Cleaning, imagine if you are thinking, "These impressions have to go! My boyfriend has disappointed me, and all of this anger I am feeling has to go out from my back!" With such a forceful approach, you will struggle, because when you try to remove a specific thing by force, you will actually deepen its effect. The moment you sit with the idea that "This *must* go," you will make it worse.

There is a more relaxed, subtler way to do it: sit peacefully and first create a prayerful state deep within your heart. Then offer the suggestion so lightly that there is as little force as possible behind it: "My Lord, may this be removed." It is a prayerful suggestion, deep in the heart. This is another reason why prayer is so important—as we master the art of prayer, the more potent our subtle power will become to bring about change.

If we are forceful, with the thought that, "This and this *must* go today," something will still happen, no doubt. Whether we order it, request it, make a subtle suggestion, or we are prayerful with love, something will always work, because nature always responds, but the response is always proportional to the level of subtlety used.

So when you practice Cleaning in the evening, try to go deep into your heart and be as gentle and subtle as you can with the instructions, and observe how purity simply descends when Cleaning is done.

As we go further and further in spiritual life, a time comes when no thought is needed, as things simply happen. In the beginning we go on refining ourselves, and our prayerful suggestions become more and more tender: "May this happen," "May this be removed," "May she develop courage." But then after some time we relax, as whatever has to happen will happen. Eventually we wonder, "I didn't do anything, but something happened today." That is because now we are no longer directing the work; we are simply allowing the work to flow through us.

Does this mean that we should remain idle from day one in this process of suggestion? No, we first have to learn the process, by going through the steps, in order for subtlety to develop. Start and see where it takes you. When you practice Cleaning, for example, start with the sankalpa that all complexities and impurities are going away from your back. Eventually a time will come when the moment you sit in the evening, you won't need the words. Things will just start happening.

It helps to understand suppositions. Throughout our daily activities, we continuously suppose things: "Look at his shirt. Where did he buy it?" "Oh, her dress is not so good," "My lecturer is in good spirits," "My mood is not okay today." We continuously suppose with the voice inside our head, even if we do not voice our suppositions aloud. These thinking patterns are likes and dislikes, as we discussed earlier in the book. Do they cultivate stillness?

There is a much more productive way to use the mind. Imagine if you had been there when the River Ganga started trickling down from its original source, at that initial moment. If you had walked alongside the very first drop of the first rivulet, it would have been wonderful—where it flowed, the kind of resistance it encountered, how it went around obstacles, and then ultimately arrived at the ocean. Likewise, you can observe the moment your ideas take birth in your heart and see where they go and how they affect your condition. Like a river flowing, your ideas evolve into something greater, and you can observe them flowing and evolving as they grow and expand. Witnessing your thoughts arising, and allowing them to flow through you, gently and subtly, is mindfulness, and also the first step of *Pratyahara* in Yoga. It will allow you to use the power of thought wisely.

When nothing further is explainable in words, you are lost in your own Self, and your thoughts are in osmosis with the Divine. Then the subtlest and most potent of all sankalpas is possible, as you are simply an instrument for a higher purpose.

CHAPTER 7

MEDITATION, YOGA, AND NEUROSCIENCE

Into the Unknown

Because of Transmission, we are able to dive deep during meditation very early in our practice and become profoundly absorbed in the inner state. This is known as Samadhi in Sanskrit, and is highly sought after in Yoga. It is the eighth and culminating stage in Patanjali's Ashtanga Yoga. In his Yoga Sutras, Patanjali describes the first level of Samadhi as a stone-like consciousness where we don't feel anything, where we are oblivious to what is happening because we have journeyed into parts of the mind beyond awareness. In Heartfulness, quite quickly we are able to go to subtler levels and experience the lighter, more evolved states of Samadhi. In the second state we are in a dreamlike, subconscious Samadhi, and in the third we are fully aware and absorbed simultaneously. This is known as *Sahaj Samadhi.*

Sahaj Samadhi is a condition of deep absorption in meditation while at the same time being fully conscious of everything that is going on. In the Yoga Shastras this is known as

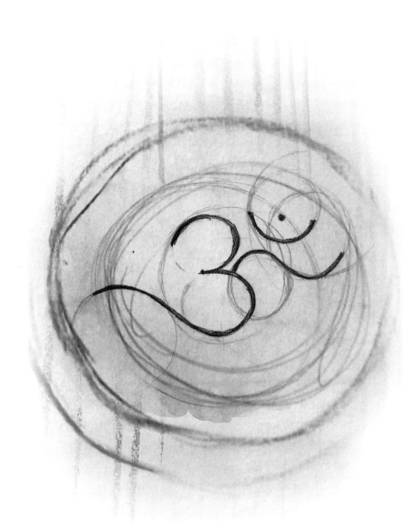

the *Turiya* condition, or the fourth state. Everything is in view. We can also continue this state during the day, while we are busy doing other things. We are simultaneously focusing on work, on the surroundings, on the TV, on something happening outside, and still remaining in communion with our inner spiritual state, on the Transmission, the condition that is prevailing within, something that is about to come into our system, thoughts that arise, and the next step we should be taking. We remain peaceful, seeing all of these things at the same moment. In Yoga this is known as the *Turiyatit* state, where we have 360-degree consciousness with eyes open. There is no need to focus on any particular thing. The moment we focus on one thing, it is no longer meditation but concentration.

Aum and Neuroscience

We can understand these various stages both from the perspectives of Yoga and neuroscience. In Yoga, *Aum* is the original sound that was manifested at the time of creation. And that sound is still there in our innate memory within the soul, starting from A to U to M and, finally, the emptiness that follows the M. It is the soundless sound that follows the M that we must capture. These three sounds and the soundless sound that follows have tremendous significance, as it is the empty silence that follows the sound of Aum that reminds us of the fourth state, or Turiya.

These states of consciousness are experienced every day by all of us, and can also be measured with an EEG machine:

1. The alert, wakeful states are characterized by brainwaves of higher frequencies:
    Gamma waves, 31–120 hertz, occur with hyper brain activity such as learning and problem solving.
    Beta waves, 13–30 hertz, occur when we are active in conversation and other activities.
    Alpha waves, 8–12 hertz, occur when we are relaxed, contemplative, absorbed in a beautiful piece of music, or when we are starting to meditate.
2. The dream state is characterized by theta waves, 4–7 hertz, and occurs when we are drowsy and drifting into sleep and dreams.
3. The deep sleep state is characterized by delta waves, 0.5–3 hertz.

In the wakeful states, consciousness is moving outward, away from the Source in search of knowledge, from which is born the field of modern science. When the brainwave frequencies become slower, it shows that we are turning inward and moving into deeper states of consciousness. The consciousness of the dream state is somewhere between the waking and sleeping state, where we dream of *slokas*, poetry, *ghazals*, etc. It is all about the inner search and is related to the inner world. In the deep-sleep state, consciousness gravitates toward its Source, the soul.

You may be familiar with the scientific research that has been done in the West on meditators practicing Transcendental Meditation, various Buddhist systems, and mindfulness. They have conducted experiments on monks and ordinary people, new meditators as well as experienced meditators who have done ten- to twenty-thousand hours of meditation.

In research studies, meditators have experienced delta frequencies, normally found during deep sleep, the dream-like theta frequencies, the relaxed alpha states, and spikes of high-frequency gamma brainwaves in patterns not normally associated with wakeful states. In fact, in yogis who meditate regularly, gamma oscillations were found to be much more common and significantly greater in amplitude than in other groups. So the spectrum of brainwave frequencies expanded in both directions as a result of meditation.

The brainwave spectrum of the Turiya state encompasses the full range of the spectrum, even that of deep sleep, or *sushupti,* indicated by delta waves, although the person meditating is simultaneously completely aware. Yogis and monks crave this state with all their might, and sometimes meditate for thousands of hours, performing penances and practices in order to reach it.

With the help of Transmission, it becomes quite easy to experience this Turiya state. Even if you have never ever meditated in your life, when you are exposed to Heartfulness Meditation with Transmission, your consciousness awakens at a different level so that you expand into the Turiya condition. While your body is fully relaxed, your mind perceives things. You are not sleeping, but you are in a relaxed state that is as rejuvenating as deep sleep. That is the true Turiya condition.

And then we learn how to take this condition out into daily life with eyes open. We transcend Turiya to the Turiyatit state. The Turiya state is available only when we are in meditation, whereas the Turiyatit state emerges when we carry that deep meditative state within us all the time. It encompasses all the states: A, U, M, and the soundless sound.

We transcend
from A, the external wakeful state,
to U, the inner dream-like state,
to M, the deep-sleep state of sushupti,
to the soundless silence of the Turiya state,
and, finally, to the Turiyatit condition.

So while it is good to be actively meditating regularly, it is even better to be in a meditative state, all the time. We are actively meditating every morning and meditatively active all the time. We actually don't have to do much except close our eyes and be receptive.

CHAPTER 8

GUIDANCE

The Guide

A GOOD TEACHER or guide is a blessing in any field of learning, because they help us to master a subject. We know it from experience, so it doesn't need an explanation. Still, it is interesting to note that there is something called coherence, where the teacher and the student resonate with each other, and a heart to heart osmosis happens in which skills and knowledge are transferred. In fact, scientists are now realizing that much more is transferred and transmitted heart-to-heart than they'd previously thought, just as happens between a mother and her children.

In worldly disciplines, those who excel know that they have to keep learning and moving forward if they are to stay ahead of the game in their profession or skill. The greatest athletes and sports stars have coaches to maintain peak performance; peer review in cutting-edge academic research is a natural part of the process of publication of a book or an article; and the best musicians in the world continue to learn from one another so as to keep improving their skills. Anyone who is really good at what they do wants guidance and feedback. That is the evolutionary approach to learning and life. And the further we go in any field, the more important it is to have a guide to help us move forward on the path. This is even more important in the spiritual field, where we are constantly venturing into new, unexplored areas, so the Guide is an important person in the life of a spiritual seeker.

What is the significance of having a living Guide, or Guru, and how do we utilize their presence? In the very early days of Heartfulness, in the early 20th century, there were only around two hundred followers, and hardly five or ten of them would be with Lalaji at any given time. One-to-one interactions were very easy, as in the ancient traditions of *gurukula* in India and Socratic learning in the West. In ancient times, students lived with their Guide for certain periods of time in order to be trained, just as Christ's disciples lived with him.

But there are now over a million people practicing Heartfulness around the world. So how will everyone spend personal time with their Guides? In order to adapt to modern times, the whole Heartfulness system has evolved so that our spiritual progress continues without requiring the actual physical presence of the Guide.

But if you do have an opportunity to visit the Guide or attend a meditation session with him, something magical happens, as you both sit with eyes closed in meditation. He does thorough cleaning, prepares you for the spiritual journey, triggers the start of the journey, and also prepares the ground ahead for where you are going. So a few things happen in his presence.

This process is optimized and accelerated if you have prepared yourself ahead of time to make the most of the opportunity. And then afterward, if your craving is of such an order that you can invite his spiritual essence to come to you, then the journey from one level to another starts.

There are so many misunderstandings about the relationship between the Heartfulness Guide and a seeker. Some people think they have to personally be with him for there to be any benefit, but it is better to close your eyes in meditation and wrap him inside your heart. Unless you interiorize his spiritual presence in your heart, being with him will be of no use anyway. The physical presence of a living Guide can be of great benefit if you have interiorized his presence and resonate in tune with him. Then you will discover that the external and the internal are the same.

It also helps to have an affectionate relationship with the Guide so that love develops. The type of sentimental relationship you have depends on your life's experiences. You may consider him as your grandfather, father, mother, friend, or Guru. His help is always there. Please try it and see the result. Invoking his presence is good enough. If you thoughtfully invoke him, asking for help, it will be there.

I can think of so many personal examples of this. There have been many times when there were irreversible situations in my life, when I would think to myself, "No, this is a dead end; there is no rescue anymore." Then, automatically, my attention would move toward my Guide. My heart would start beating faster and, surprisingly, the problems simply disappeared as if a miracle had taken place.

Then, after four or five experiences like that, I started to feel, "Enough of these miracles." I became tired of experiences and miracles, and the feeling that remained was, "I want to *become* like him."

A time comes when we want to become like the Guide. Now does that mean we should become like him in physical appearance? No, there is no need to grow a beard because he has a beard, wear similar clothes, or eat the foods he likes. That will not take us anywhere. What works is to try to emulate his attitude, his practice, his etiquette, and his relationship with his Guide.

When we read Babuji's diaries as a disciple of Lalaji, it both humbles and motivates us. He writes that he did a few things simultaneously. These I have tried to emulate and found them very useful:

1. Always remain connected through your heart with your Guide.
2. Adjust yourself with your present inner condition and try to absorb it and deepen it.
3. Prepare for the condition that is to come next; wait for it, anticipate it, and look forward to it.
4. Always be vigilant about your surroundings: What must you be doing?

When Babuji later became Lalaji's successor, all of these things happened together, and his eyes also had 360-degree global vision: "What is happening with this seeker, that seeker, this continent, that continent?" The human mind has so many channels, and it can do so many things at one time.

The Guide is not God. When we think like that, we bring religion into the spiritual world. No doubt he is Godly in nature, but he is not God. We are also trying to become Godly; that is our endeavor in Heartfulness. We don't become the Guide, but we can become like the Guide in his inner attributes and qualities.

Another misunderstanding is that the Guide is there to solve all our worldly and emotional problems. Heartfulness is all about taking those problems into our own hands and solving them for ourselves. Heartfulness teaches us how to do that. It prepares us from within, and it strengthens us in such a way that we become masters of our lives. That is why our Guides have said again and again, "We don't make disciples; we make masters." By mastering our lives, we learn how to live smoothly and peacefully and go gracefully toward our goal.

How lightly this journey has to be taken up! When even the self is nonexistent, where is there room for problems? If we remain focused on problems, we will gravitate more and more toward them. When the self is nonexistent, where is there room even for bliss? We move beyond all of these things.

What About God?

Some of us believe in God; others do not. It actually does not matter when you approach Heartfulness from the perspective of personal experience. A person who does not believe in God generally says, "I have not experienced God, so how can I believe?" and those who do believe in God generally do not have personal experience upon which to base that claim.

If you ask anyone, "Have you experienced God yourself, or do you believe in God because your parents or your priest say God exists?" they will generally say it is because others believe, not because they have any personal experience of God.

So how do we rise above this to experience God?

The Heartfulness approach is scientific, so you are welcome to start either with God's existence or nonexistence in your experiment. Then, in a scientific way, you can observe within and come to your own conclusion. The results of practice will affirm the efficacy of the system to your heart. If you are on the wrong path, your heart will immediately tell you. If you are on the right path and the experience satisfies your heart, it's a positive signal to proceed further. As you proceed, you come across so many varying states of consciousness— meditative and nonmeditative states, peaceful and not-so-peaceful states, etc.—and you will become cognizant, pushing you to trust the meditative states more and more.

Gradually you learn the art of remaining in the meditative state in all your day-to-day activities, and this happens whether you are a believer in God or a nonbeliever. For a believer, the journey is easier, since it is a positive approach. The negative approach, like many other negative things in life, is always difficult to circumvent. Nevertheless, this practice ensures that nonbelief soon transmutes into a heartfelt positive signal of the subtle presence of the higher Being.

After all, you will be convinced of the existence of God when you experience Divinity within yourself during meditation and when you become more and more Godly in your own person. Then you can confidently say, "Yes, I know now that God exists," and there will be substance to it.

I often give the analogy of currencies. There are so many currencies worldwide, and they are supposedly backed by resources, such as gold, silver, oil, minerals, and nowadays even political stability. The more resources and stability the country has, the stronger the currency. On what backing are we claiming that God exists? If we don't have the backing of experience, it is no different from saying that God does not exist.

Through meditation, first we have a temporary experience of peace, calmness, stillness, and bliss. For a moment we seem to lose ourselves in something unknown; we don't know what it is. It is pleasant, but it is temporary. We might think, "Maybe this is the Godly experience, but we are not so sure about it." Eventually a more tangible proof of God's existence within happens when that experience becomes more and more frequent, and then permanent. This process is greatly aided by the Transmission flowing from the Source into our hearts during Meditation. This can really only be understood well through personal experience.

To use another worldly analogy, there is no point becoming a millionaire for a month. Let's say somebody says, "I will lend you one hundred million dollars today, and after one month I will take it back." It is just like saying, "While I was visiting my Guide, I had a great experience, a superb experience, but afterward I was not able to keep that spiritual state." Are we like the millionaire who loses his or her millions after a month? After we leave the atmosphere of our Guide's presence, will we again be "high and dry," spiritually speaking?

When we return home after being with the Guide, we will meditate and have experiences. At times they may be intense, and at other times they may not be so fulfilling. When our meditation loses its intensity, we usually ask a trainer, "Please can I have a meditation session with you? My condition seems to have gone away. I would like to regain my connection with God, with my inner Self." So we meditate with a trainer, we feel the flame alive in our heart, and again we feel God within. But then, after some time, again it fizzles out. So we are constantly connecting and disconnecting ourselves. Ideally, we want that experience of connection to become permanent.

Why do we have such beautiful experiences? What is the purpose? Where do they take us? When we are in deep meditation, for hours we don't know what is happening, we are so lost. It is like intoxication. At the same time it is such a pleasant condition. But is it necessary? At each stage, experiences are bound to arise. It is not that the Guide gives them to us or God gives them to us. When a train is moving, let us say from Rome toward Paris, the change in scenery reminds us that we are moving, that we are progressing. That is one reason for having different experiences when we sit for meditation—to give us confidence. Otherwise, if we go on continuously experiencing the same thing, we will lose interest.

This happens especially at the earlier stages of our inner journey. There are an infinite number of experiences we can have while we are journeying through the chakras associated with worldly existence, which are found in the chest area, known as the Heart Region, or *Pind Pradesh*. After this, the Guide moves us into another galaxy, the higher chakras associated with various parts of the head. Here we are no longer in the world of duality, of worldly existence. We are in a whole new dimension. This journey through the chakras, known as the *yatra*, describes our progress and our expansion of consciousness, and we will return to it later on.

PART II

LIFESTYLE

Externalize the change.

CHAPTER 9

TRANSFORM YOUR SELF

AFTER STARTING HEARTFULNESS practice, many of us feel a lot of inner change. Our consciousness expands, old habits and reactions drop off, and we become more aware of our place in the world. We are drawn to simplify our lifestyle also, as things that once seemed so important lose their glamour and enticement. But lifestyle transformation also demands alertness and some active cooperation, as it is not all automatic. We need to refine our thoughts, emotions, behavior, and attitudes.

I would like to share with you some of the wisdom Heartfulness has to offer in improving and refining our lifestyle. These practices and approaches have worked so well for me. The first thing is to want to change and then to create a direction for that change. This starts by having an intention.

Intention

To achieve anything in life, whether worldly or spiritual in nature, we must first simplify our intention. There is a story from my youth that explains it beautifully.

Back in the late 1970s, I was sitting with my first Guide, Babuji, on his verandah. It was a wintry morning in December in Shahjahanpur, northern India. He was alone, and I was seated in a corner.

He gestured to me, saying, "Come," so I went and sat near him. He scratched a white line on his hand with his finger-nail, and it made a mark on his skin because it was so cold.

I wondered what Babuji was doing.

He said, "This is a water canal."

It was like a make-believe game. Then, from the same canal, he scratched his hand again and drew another line, so that the canal was divided into two streams.

"You understand?"

I said, "What, Babuji?"

"Fifty percent of the power is reduced."

Then he scratched himself again, producing a third canal.

"Now do you understand?"

I said, "Yes, Babuji."

The power was further reduced.

Taking an everyday example, how many applications do you have on your phone? If you leave them all running, the battery drains very quickly. In life, if you run too many appli-cations, you also drain yourself very quickly, and you are not happy with one focus.

This principle applies in all fields, including career, relation-ships, and self-development. Having one application, one goal, takes you somewhere, through the optimum utilization of inner resources. This ability to focus on one goal develops naturally out of meditative practice, as we learn to simplify our thought process from scattered to focused. It is known as

Dharana in Yoga, which is the sixth limb of Patanjali's Ashtanga Yoga. We regulate our mind and refine our consciousness.

But this is not the final outcome. Over time we go much further than this in Heartfulness Meditation. It leads us to 360-degree consciousness, enabling us to focus on all aspects of daily life plus the inner state at the same time. So it is not about running away from life. It simply means that our life's main purpose is clear; it is evolutionary, and everything else that happens slowly moves in tune with that purpose.

Simplicity of intention is strengthened by practicing the Heartfulness Prayer. Every day we are reminded of our inner goal—it sets our direction like the rudder of a ship. Because we go deep inside and listen to the heart, we learn to integrate the inside and outside, and that is the key to self-mastery.

Then we can be playing soccer, driving, cooking dinner, reading a story to our children, or running a business, and all the while still have an underlying focus on our inner state. Our consciousness can be in osmosis there while we happily attend to other things.

With this clarity of mind, it is easy to sail smoothly through life and the infinite ocean of the inner journey with the right understanding. That is how we weave our destiny.

To be happy, our inner and outer states need to be in harmony, otherwise we feel unsettled and unbalanced. We cannot be true to ourselves if what we feel on the inside and what we are on the outside are not in sync. As Polonius said to his son, Laertes, in Shakespeare's *Hamlet*:

This above all: to thine own self be true,
And it must follow, as the night the day,
Thou canst not then be false to any man.

Listen to Your Heart

The heart is a barometer of how we feel about everything, including ourselves—how we feel about our thoughts and emotions, our behavior, and about the choices we make in life. If we are happy, then we will not hear from the heart. When we are about to choose well, the heart simply remains a silent witness to the decision we are contemplating. There is natural contentment. When we are not happy with ourselves, the heart is restless. It lets us know that something needs to change.

Listening to the heart's signals is the first step. The second step is to make use of those signals, to ask the heart questions in such a way that we get clear indications. Slowly we get the hang of it, and the more we listen the clearer the messages become. When we don't listen, we lose the art of listening to the heart. Neuroscientists describe it as losing the neural circuitry or pathways that we do not use. Then it takes a lot of effort to reactivate them. The more we use the neural pathways, the stronger they become.

Now comes the third step: having listened to the voice of the heart, do we have the courage to follow it?

You probably know the story of Pinocchio, whose nose grew longer every time he lied. It is easy to tell a white lie to avoid conflict and unpleasantness, but what happens to our heart when we do? It starts pumping fast. When purity is compromised, the heart becomes heavy and anxious. Then what takes over? Discomfort, followed by guilt and regret. We start disliking ourselves: "How could I have done such a thing!"

Sometimes people lie to please their parents, or to avoid hurting another person, but even then, instead of lightness, joy, and confidence in our heart, we still often feel compromised. There are situations, however, where our heart chooses to put relationships above truthfulness as an ethical choice, avoiding danger or trouble. For example, what happens when we need to protect someone we love? There is quite a famous case of this in a painting, depicting a small boy during the Second World War being questioned by soldiers about the whereabouts of his parents. Of course he knew his parents were hiding in the cellar under the floorboards, but he also knew that if he told the soldiers, they would kill his parents. What would you do in this situation? Tell the truth or protect your parents? Again, it is your heart that will guide you. This art of listening to the heart brings contentment; we feel integrated, whole, and at peace with ourselves as a result.

Learning to listen to the heart is one thing, but there is an added dimension to this process: our heart is not static. Our inner environment is constantly changing as we expand and refine our consciousness, or restrict our consciousness, as the case may be. The field of consciousness is fluid, so the reference point of the heart is dynamic. And everything about us is tied to our state of consciousness: the food we eat, the clothes we wear, the habits that slowly adjust to our changing level of evolution. We are always in a state of continuous improvement, a work in progress.

But it happens that sometimes we choose to go against our conscience, because our desires and mental justifications push us to make another choice. And until we change our thinking, we will keep on recycling those experiences and habits. So what do we do? There is always a choice. We can either do nothing, or we can choose to rectify the situation. There is a very effective Heartfulness practice we can do:

Let Go of Burdens

At bedtime, feel the divine presence in your heart, and repent for anything you have done wrong, even if unintentional. There is no recrimination in this process.

While deep in your heart, prayerfully resolve not to make the same mistake again. You will feel as if a burden has lifted.

You can also present any questions and confusions to your heart right after offering prayer. There is no need to seek an answer right away. Often, by the time you wake up, you will know the answer. Even if the answer comes in another form than words, you will surely have the solution.

Managing Emotions

Even when we have established a regular Heartfulness practice, more often than not we still struggle with emotional reactions to the ups and downs of daily life. Some days we feel calm with the world around us, while on other days we feel angry, anxious, upset, overexcited, or fearful. When we observe the patterns our emotional lives follow, we notice that there are certain cyclical rhythms in the ups and downs.

How can we work with emotions and reactions so that our lives are more in tune with a calm, inner meditative state? Yogic psychology provides us with such a beautiful and sophisticated way of understanding and refining our emotions, and this work complements the inner spiritual work.

Emotions and Feelings Arise in the Heart

The first thing we observe through meditation is that emotions and feelings arise in the heart. We feel things in the heart, not with our intellect or reasoning ability. While these feelings and emotions then affect our thinking process, especially through the limbic system of the midbrain, the initial impulses arise in the heart.

Not all of us are comfortable exploring the inner world of our feelings, simply because we have not been encouraged to do so as we were growing up, either at home or at school. Is it the physical heart that feels? No. It is the vibratory or energetic heart, also known as the subtle body. There is so much talk today of emotional intelligence, as defined by Daniel Goleman in his famous book, including the heart-based qualities of compassion, empathy, resilience, love, courage, and will, and these qualities are not physical in nature. They reside in the vibratory heart, which is where we also find the chakras of the heart. But whenever the vibratory heart is affected in any way, this then affects the physical heart. For example, if we become angry, our heart rate variability becomes erratic and our blood pressure goes up, even though the origin of the emotion is in the subtle body. So to improve our emotional intelligence, we need to work with the subtle body through the heart.

Emotions versus Feelings

The second thing we observe is the difference between emotions and feelings, especially as a result of the Cleaning process. Feelings are like pure fire without any smoke, where the wood burns clear and pure. Emotions are clouded or filtered, like fire with a lot of smoke due to dampness or impurities in the wood. And the purest feelings of all are like electricity, where there is not even any burning. Pure feelings are natural and helpful for our evolution, whereas emotions are clouded by impurities, just like smoky wood. What causes the impurities? The impressions, or samskaras, that settle in the heart that we spoke about earlier: the purer the heart, the clearer the feelings.

Feelings, Emotions, and the Chakras of the Heart

The third thing we observe is that the heart chakra consists broadly of five different energy centers, or chakras, associated with the five traditional elements of life: earth, space, fire, water, and air. These five elements are known in Yoga as the *pancha bhutas,* and each one has a particular spectrum of emotions and feelings that we master as we travel on our inner journey. In fact, feelings and emotions collect in the human system in quite a specific way, which we can map in our spiritual anatomy. Unless and until we master these chakras through spiritual practice, we will not master the emotions associated with them. Each of the five chakras is associated with a particular duality of feeling, and the dualities are known as the *dwandwas,* or opposites.

So as we purify and traverse each chakra of the heart, removing the impressions that have lodged there, as well as mastering the feelings and emotions associated with each, step-by-step we develop greater levels of emotional intelligence and maturity. Working with the spiritual anatomy of the chakras gives us so much insight into our emotions that I will now share with you some very practical tools to master them so that we are able to let go of subconscious patterns and redesign our destinies.

Spiritual Anatomy

What creates emotional turbulence in our consciousness? In a lake of water, energy creates turbulence in the form of waves and ripples. In the lake of consciousness, energy creates turbulence in the form of thoughts, feelings, and emotions.

We have already described the formation of samskaras in the section on Heartfulness Cleaning—the formation of knots of energy that arise due to our thoughts and experience—so now we will explore how this works with respect to various feelings and emotions.

The Heart Region of a human being is the region associated with the dualities of everyday life. Every chakra has its own polarity or duality of feelings. The first chakra, or point 1 of the Heart Region, is in the lower left part of the chest where the physical heart is found. This point is associated with the element of earth, and when we meditate we may see a glimpse of the color yellow in the inner environment. The spectrum of feelings here is desire versus contentment, which can be equated with the lack of desire known as *vairagya* in Yoga. At first it seems like each spectrum has a "good" and a "bad" to it, so contentment is positive and desire is negative. In a way that is correct, as desires for worldly things pull us down and create samskaras. But as the chakra is purified and we master the emotions there, we discover that both ends of the spectrum have an evolutionary purpose.

chakras of the Heart Region.

TRANSFORM YOUR SELF | 89

Eventually, at point 1, the desire or craving for something higher propels us toward our spiritual goal while contentment brings peace, stability, and grounding in spiritual practice and poise and patience in worldly life. When we are pulled by desires for worldly possessions or sensuality, or when we are crippled by guilt, jealousy, or resentment, this chakra is clouded by desire-based impressions and becomes very heavy.

As we remove the desire-based attachments that pull us down, through Cleaning, and go deeper into the feelings and consciousness of the heart through Prayer, Meditation, and introspection, our emotions become less reactive, more and more subtle, and we eventually master the spectrum of desire and contentment associated with chakra 1 so that we can benefit both from restlessness toward the goal and contentment.

The second chakra, point 2 of the Heart Region, is on the lower right side of the chest. This is the soul chakra, where the element is ether, also known as space or *akasha*, and we glimpse the color red. At this point, we find so much peace that we don't feel like doing worldly things. Whether a businessman, a student, or a stay-at-home parent, we lose interest in everything for some time, because peace is so inviting and we do not want to be disturbed or distracted from it. That is the quality of the second point.

The spectrum of feelings here is from anxiety or restlessness to peace. When the heart is clouded by samskaras, when we still carry a lot of heaviness at the first point of the heart, all that heaviness will evaporate to the second point. Then there can be no peace at the second point, because we feel anxious and worried. Instead we continually get pulled back into worldly entanglements, and the peace and joy of the soul eludes us. There are four main satellite points around chakra 1, known as A, B, C, and D, which are the points where impressions enter and first lodge in our system. (We will describe them in more detail shortly.) If these four points are kept healthy, and surrounded with a cleaner inner atmosphere, to the same extent we will not pollute our other chakras.

The third chakra, or point 3 of the Heart Region, is on the upper left side of the chest. This is the fire point, where we may glimpse the color white during meditation. The feelings at this chakra are more passionate and inspirational in nature, and the spectrum is that of anger versus love. We experience them according to the impressions and desires we hold: when anger and love are clouded by worldly desires, either one can pull us down into emotional entanglements, but when they are pure, both of them can propel us further on our journey.

Let's start with love. Love for God and for the Guide blossom at this point, as we feel more and more gratitude for the inner progress we have experienced. Love fuels our journey, propelling us upward like a rocket. We start to develop an intense attachment to God and to the Guide who is taking us on this journey. Love takes us upward, just as a flame always points upward, burning everything else that hampers our progress. At chakra 3, the fire point, love is awakened toward the divine Source so that it transcends everyday human love and becomes alchemical in nature.

In its pure expression, anger is also uplifting and transformative. It is an evolutionary tool gifted to us for self-refinement, and is known in Yoga as *krodha,* one of the two divine emotions. It is a change agent, a natural warning sign that something needs to change. When we feel angry, an important step is to acknowledge that the change needs to happen within ourselves.

Unfortunately, most of us take our anger out on others, aggressively and forcefully, or we repress it inwardly in an unhealthy way, leading to depression. Those approaches are not helpful. But as we journey through chakra 3, we have the possibility to master anger and harness it for our evolution and onward journey. It becomes such a wonderful tool for change when we utilize it in a healthy way.

When love and anger are thus refined at point 3, this experience then translates to the next duality at point 4, on the upper right side of the chest. Courage and fear are the dual qualities of point 4. The more we are able to purify and ennoble love and anger at point 3, the better the quality of courage and fear we will have. This is the water point, where we may glimpse the color black, and the spectrum of feelings runs like the deep current of water, encompassing fear and courage.

When the heart is not yet pure, we tend to view fear as a negative emotion and courage as a positive emotion. Fear is associated with particular events, people, or situations from our past—for example, fear of snakes, fear of flying, fear of public speaking, fear of being alone in the dark, and fear of losing a person or thing. Fear is associated with our past experiences, and it can be heavy and crippling, leading to terror, stunting our confidence, and stifling our interest.

But when the heart is pure, fear is also pure and natural, and this "real fear" is the natural caution that encourages us to be careful, to develop self-discipline, to conserve our resources, and to stay on the path we have chosen. When we cultivate healthy caution as a quality, we don't take anything for granted. This naturally leads to reverence and respect for all life forms, and gratitude and etiquette toward others in daily life.

How are Samskaras formed?

Thought → Action → Habit → Impression

Inaction → Guilt

At the opposite end of the spectrum is courage. Generally we think of courage as something very positive, as it is needed to move forward and develop confidence, even on the spiritual journey. But without fear as a counterbalance, courage can be reckless and can fuel the ego, leading to arrogance. Imagine a murderer or a thief with unlimited courage! So as the heart is purified and we traverse chakra 4, we learn to use both fear and courage for our evolution and advancement.

The love that has awakened at chakra 3 deepens at chakra 4 into something subtler, less passionate, and stronger, creating the foundation for courage. Just like in a marriage, the initial outer expression of love becomes subtler and deeper as love matures.

The fifth chakra, or point 5 of the Heart Region, is also known as the throat chakra in the older yogic traditions, and is the air point of the Heart Region. Here we may glimpse the color green, and the spectrum we experience here is from illusion and confusion at one end to clarity and wisdom at the other. When the field of consciousness in the heart is pure, the air element brings great clarity and wisdom, whereas confusion and illusion are an indication that there is turbulence. When this is the case it is an indication to pause and wait for clarity to come before making any decision. Confusion at point 5 is more likely to occur if there is any heaviness at points A, B, C, and D around chakra 1 of the heart, which then evaporates to points 2, 3, and 4 as well. When the heart is pure, each of these dualities helps to propel us forward on our journey through the Heart Region, and take us to the next stage, where we eventually transcend them all.

But for most of us, the heart is filled with accumulated complexities and impurities, and we continue to create more of them day by day. This is why we react so easily and get caught up in the entanglements of emotions. How are these impressions created? It all starts with simple wishes, likes, and dislikes. These then lead to desires, both positive and negative. All our desires, including the negative ones of aversion, arise in the heart and lead to impressions settling at the various satellite energy centers or points around chakra 1 of the Heart Region—points A, B, C, and D.

Points A, B, C, and D

We are constantly playing with likes and dislikes in our hearts, and they affect our thinking, often without us realizing it. When we like certain things and dislike others, if those responses stay in our emotional field, they settle at point C near point 1 on the lower left side of the chest area. This is the strategic point in our spiritual anatomy, as it is the landing point for impressions to enter our system. From point C the impressions gravitate toward various other satellite points near point 1 of the heart. This is because different emotions have different vibrations. For example, worldly worries settle at point A, sensuality and sexual desire settle at point B, and guilt settles at point D.

When we worry about our worldly problems and brood over them, it affects point A. None of us can escape worries. Actually, when we worry about challenges, it is a good indication that we have to act upon our concerns and solve the problems, and finding solutions strengthens our self-confidence and mental faculties. Whereas when we keep on worrying perpetually without solving the problems as they arise, it is only going to make it worse and create heaviness at point A.

Points A, B, C, D & point - 1

Ribcage Cavity   2f   *A - 1
                    1f   B
                           C D
              4f   2f

Another part of human existence is our sexuality and sensual attraction toward others. When it is balanced and in moderation it is manageable, but when it overwhelms us, those impressions form at point B.

There is another emotion that creates deep impressions, and that is guilt. Guilt is perhaps the heaviest impression we can form. It arises out of something we did not do but should have done, or something we did but should not have done. Guilt gives rise to a lot of heaviness in the heart and settles at point D.

These points A to D are satellites around point 1 of the heart. They are only four subpoints of the thousands of subpoints in our spiritual anatomy, but they are four major ones that go on collecting impressions.

To find them, use your fingers to measure the distances as follows:

1. First, find the cavity at the base of the ribcage, in the middle, where the two halves meet.

2. Then measure one finger-width downward.

3. Then measure four fingers-width horizontally in a straight line toward the left side of the chest. This is point B.

4. Two fingers straight above that is point A.

5. Straight below point B, touching the lowest rib is point C.

6. Two fingers-width horizontal toward the left side is point D.

7. The nipple should be straight above. The midpoint between point D and the left nipple is point 1, the *Hridaya* chakra.

Why am I sharing this knowledge with you? So that you can start to be aware. When you observe what happens at points A, B, C, and D around your heart, you will notice that they are activated when you feel any of the associated emotions. When you notice emotions, you have an opportunity to adjust yourself and clean yourself, instead of judging and reacting. Try to observe your emotions with an attitude of self-acceptance. Without it, it is difficult to graciously let go of impressions, because instead you will end up thinking about them, or feeling bad about yourself, deepening the impressions. You will need self-acceptance to get to first base!

When these impressions are removed by Cleaning, you will no longer be bothered as much by desires, and the result is contentment. When the impressions continue to create heaviness, you will remain disturbed.

The state of purity or impurity at these points A, B, C, and D has a ripple effect outward on the rest of your system. When there is purity, it evaporates to point 2 of the Heart Region, and when point 2 is pure it is full of peace. Now, when you feel a continuous vibration of peace from a person or a situation in life, what happens? It is very easy to love that person or situation, whereas if they go on creating disturbances or complexities all the time, you become irritated instead.

And that is experienced at point 3, on the upper left side of the chest. Here anger and love are perpetually present. And as love and anger are purified, then at point 4 courage and strength automatically develop, as well as a healthy fear to keep you on track. The experience at point 4 gives rise to the qualities of point 5 at the throat; purity, clarity, and wisdom are associated with this chakra.

This butterfly effect continues to affect the higher points, from point 6 upward in the Mind Region. The Mind Region actually cannot tolerate illusion, so when the mind is disturbed by heaviness and complexity, we lose our humanity, our human traits. That is why the first step in any inner journey is to clean the heart of all the impressions that have formed in our system. Otherwise, it is not possible to tolerate the load of heaviness and, at the same time, continue to proceed on the journey. It would be like climbing Mount Everest with 10 kg of concrete attached to each shoe. The trick is to be courageous, loving, peaceful, and less inviting to desires.

Heartfulness Practices for Points A, B, C, and D

In Heartfulness, we not only observe these points A to D, we also have practices to refine and purify them, as follows:

Preventing Likes and Dislikes at Point C

Everything starts at point C, the strategic point or landing point for samskaras into our system. As we have already discussed, it is our reactions of likes and dislikes that create the first vibration or stir in the field of consciousness. This affects point C, and from there the energy forms an impression.

> To prevent impressions from settling at point C, try to maintain a meditative state throughout the day so that the mind is not pulled by likes and dislikes. If this is done, impressions will not affect the field of consciousness. This is one of the most important things we can do for our mental and spiritual health, and it highlights the importance of maintaining a meditative state during the day.

But, sometimes, impressions do form in our system, and when they do we also have the following practices to remove them:

Meditate for Unity on Point A

We meditate on point A to promote a feeling of universal brotherhood, leading to unity among all. This meditation is to be done before the bedtime prayer for five to seven minutes.

- For men: Fix your attention on Point A, with the thought that all the women and men of the world are your sisters and brothers. Hold your thought on this while you meditate on Point A, believing this to be true. If practiced wholeheartedly you can see its effect immediately, and this effect will be permanent.

- For women: Think that all divine gifts are available to you, and that all men and women of the world think they are brothers and sisters and your thought is one with theirs.

Why are there different practices for men and women? If you introspect on this, you will begin to see that the difference reflects the difference between Yin and Yang, the feminine and masculine polarity or complementarity. When you let this understanding unfold, it will reveal much about why there are two sexes, and how we complement and teach each other.

If this practice were done daily by people around the world, then the idea of one human family would become a reality very quickly. All resentment, jealousy, personal conflicts, worldly conflicts, possessiveness, and greed would evaporate, and unity would prevail. Such a simple, effective tool has been given to us to manage our worldly worries and bring about oneness.

Manage Sensual Desires at Point B

This process is to be done when you wake in the morning, before your morning Meditation; again only for five to seven minutes.

> Fix your attention on Point B and imagine that all impurities and heaviness are going out of Point B from the front of the body. Imagine that as this process is going on, the glow of the soul begins to appear from behind.

The second divine emotion is *kama*, or passion, and we know that it is necessary for procreation so that the human species continues. God was not a fool to create two sexes, but just as celibacy is not the natural state, at the other extreme passion can also get out of hand and end up in sex addiction or perversion. So this creative energy needs to be managed and balanced. For this purpose, the cleaning of point B works as a passion detox or sex detox, balancing this energy so that we are not overwhelmed by sensual desires. Imagine the harmony that would result in human societies if people around the world practiced it daily!

These Heartfulness methods of Point A Meditation and Point B Cleaning have been developed to remove the heavier tendencies in our life. By practicing them daily, you will contribute toward your own purification as well as to the greater good.

Let Go of Guilt at Point D

Guilt is the heaviest of all the impressions we carry, and it bothers us a lot. Our thoughts, feelings, and actions may create guilt, but our inactions may create even worse guilt. Lost opportunities haunt us: "If I had studied a little more, I would have been admitted to college. My career would have been . . . ," or "If only I had not said something mean to my father before he left for work this morning," or "If I had been more thoughtful and caring, perhaps my daughter would not have left home."

Inaction is serious business. Suppose a doctor is making the rounds of a hospital and a lady is vomiting. She says, "I will come back in ten minutes, as I have to see some other patients. Nurse, look after her." But when the doctor comes back, the patient is dead. Would she sleep that night knowing she could have done something?

When we go to bed at night, the thoughts that come to mind first are often about those things we missed. Sometimes they wake us in the middle of the night. "I forgot my grandmother's birthday!" or "I promised my daughter we would spend time together this evening, but I was having drinks with my colleagues after work and the time flew by!" Things we don't do create heavy impressions that turn to guilt. That guilt stays at the deepest levels of our system and is the heaviest and most difficult impression to remove.

To remove guilt, we need a commitment of a very high order and cooperation at every level. We have to face the guilt and expose ourselves, becoming naked from inside. By opening our hearts, we can say to the Lord or to our Guide, "I have created all this. I will not do it again, but please help me remove this." The important thing is to make a sincere resolve not to repeat the same thought or action again in the future.

The best time to do this is before sleeping at night. When we let go of guilt at this time, imagine the positive effect it will have on our sleep! We do not need to remember all the things we did wrong, because when we open ourselves, the Guide will remove what he has to remove. There will be many such sessions, over which time his help will gradually dissolve the heaviness.

When we meditate with Transmission, guilt will surely surface to be removed. It is precisely because of the work our Guide is doing that these thoughts have come to the surface to leave, so why hide them? There is no point struggling with thoughts. Once we know the mechanism of why thoughts arise in the mind, it becomes much easier to cooperate.

It happens because the Guide is vacuumizing our system; he is pulling all the complexities out. And then he fills the heart with lightness, and with the universal knowledge and the divine wisdom we require to lead a properly balanced life.

Finding Happiness

The German philosopher Schopenhauer once asked the question, "How can we determine whether a man is happy or unhappy?"

He defined true happiness as the complete satisfaction of all desires.

So we could describe the happiness of a person mathematically as:

$$\text{Happiness} = \frac{\text{Number of desires fulfilled}}{\text{Total number of desires}}$$

Say we have ten desires and five are fulfilled, then we have 50 percent happiness. If ten are fulfilled, we have 100 percent happiness. The more desires we have, the harder it will be to fulfill them all, so the less happy we will be. Happiness is inversely related to the number of desires. But what happens when we have no desires at all? The denominator becomes zero. Anything divided by zero is indeterminate, so if we have zero desires, our happiness will be limitless.

In this state of no desires, we do not expect anything, even from ourselves. When we don't expect anything, we don't play games or manipulate others. This has an important effect on how we weave our destiny. Think for a moment about how we human beings destroy our inner condition and our humanness: it all starts with desires. When desires are not fulfilled, there is disappointment. Disappointment leads to anger; anger makes us lose our balance; and once we lose our balance, our mental equilibrium, fear develops, so we are destroyed and lose our humanness.

Whatever happens in life, either the results are favorable or not favorable. Generally, when the results are favorable we are happy, and when the results are not favorable we are disturbed. If an action gives good results and it keeps happening, we develop a happy disposition. But what happens to a person who has disappointment after disappointment? That person generally stops trusting.

So how can we be happy under all circumstances, because that is the ultimate happiness. In order to have limitless happiness, limitless bliss, we need to minimize our desires, from more to less. When we are able to make peace with ourselves that way, we will feel, "Whatever happens, I am happy."

Cleaning impressions at the end of each day also helps. We are able to loosen the pull of desires and keep a joyful disposition.

Now, is it possible to lead a life without any desires? No one can live without desires. It is how we associate our desires with emotions that makes the difference. For example, children need to have toys for their development, but that can lead to the desire to have more and more toys. It is okay for a child to play with toys, but when adults are still playing with remote cars or Barbie dolls, it is foolish. Likewise, when young adults desire romance it is okay, but when older people still flirt, then it is counterproductive at many levels—physical, mental, emotional, and spiritual. So even for the same person at different ages, their level of emotional maturity will affect how they manifest desires.

It is perfectly okay to want to marry the right person, to want to succeed in business to support a family, to want to work in a good environment, and to want a good education in a reputed university. If desires can be translated into aspirations, then they are evolutionary. It is when desires drag us down into the whirlpool of multiple desires that heaviness is created in our system. When desires are aspirational it leads to "becoming" and "being," as opposed to only having and fulfilling desires.

So how do we solve the riddle of living with desires and not letting them affect us? There is no easy answer, but a state of contentment will prevail in us due to our practice. As a result, we are able to have aspirational desires without getting carried away with the pulls and pushes of "haves" and "have nots." The key lies in arriving at a state of contentment. When there is totality of involvement without ego, pride, or arrogance in whatever we are doing, there is joy and contentment.

Criticism Is Good!

Criticism is a sensitive topic, as most of us don't like to be criticized, yet without it how would we change and grow? It is not easy to see ourselves as we are, so criticism is like a mirror in which other people are our reflection. Generally, in the process, the other person is also learning; they would not point out our faults if they did not also have something of the same. That is why our faults irritate them so much. They are also in the process of change, so the whole exercise is beneficial to both.

Then there is the constructive criticism of a Guide, which is designed for our evolution. Babuji once said:

> If we observe you and highlight what must be corrected in your behavior, we don't mean to play the bogeyman. A Guide cares about his aspirants; he wants the best for them. If we do not do so for you, who will? Would you accept it of your family, or your friends? We are not judgmental; there lies the difference.
>
> We want to see you all growing, divested from your dregs; our objective is very different. To alleviate your burden, to purify you and refine you in all your perceptions—including the ability to feel us by your side—all this constitutes one of the aspects of spiritual work. We want to make you stronger in the face of tests, more detached from superfluity, this superfluity that can only weigh down your process. We suggest to you positive and constructive attitudes to mold your personality. A spiritual process requires efforts on all the levels.
>
> Following a method, even if it is effective, entails a transformation of your character. It is a desirable whole, an utmost commitment, if you want to achieve the best results. It is a personal choice; we cannot do it for you.

Husbands often get annoyed when their wives point out their faults, and vice versa, but why get annoyed when they are doing our work for us? They are showing us where we need to improve. So why not be thankful instead? And if something is really not justified, then just let it go. The benefits of criticism far outweigh the disadvantages. It is a mature and wise person who graciously accepts criticism.

Excel in Everything You Do

I have often thought that the purpose of life is to excel in everything we do. Whether it is as a leader, a painter, a student or a cleaner, we can excel. In every little task there is the potential for excellence.

Sometimes we hear people say, "I don't want to excel because my ego will swell. I want to be humble, not full of ego."

It is good not to be egotistical, but not at the cost of excelling.

Your ego will only inflate when you think or say, "Look at my work. It's so wonderful. I did it. You are not as good as me."

It is best not to use the ego to hurt others, but it is well utilized when we can look inside and say, "Let me do better than I did the last time."

The ego can never be destroyed, nor should it be, as it is one of our vital instruments for evolution when used well. With a true ego, we do not compare ourselves with others. Instead we compare ourselves with our previous performance. Then the utilization of ego is productive.

The same is true of spiritual practice. How did Babuji originally receive all the methods of Meditation with Transmission, Cleaning, Prayer, points A and B, etc.? The content came as a feeling. It had to be like this: the way was shown, and the feelings were there. And then the feelings were translated into words. Babuji put those words on paper and the practices became the method. So when we practice, we are learning to reverse this process. First we read the words, then we follow the method, and eventually, those words will again become the feeling.

And when we come to a level where we do the Cleaning with that feeling, words are no longer necessary. Instead of saying, "All the impurities and complexities are going away," we start doing the Cleaning directly. But let this evolve naturally; let it come on its own as a result of practicing the words first.

Similarly, with the Prayer, many a time we start to pray and become prayerful, then we dissolve in it. Words are no longer necessary. They are there to create a state of mind, a state of heart, a state of spiritual condition. When we have that, we have transcended words.

Sometimes the same experience happens with Meditation. We don't even complete the sentence, "The source of Light in my heart . . ." By the time we close our eyes, the Transmission has started and we are lost in it. So that is the beauty of Heartfulness: although the method is there, we have not even completed the words and it starts happening.

When it is like that, we don't "do" Meditation; it happens to us. With Prayer, a state of prayer starts happening inside us. The conditions also start unfolding within us, one after the other, if we allow them to happen.

In contrast, when people say, "I do my Meditation regularly before sunrise, and as soon as I come home I do Cleaning, I never miss it, and before I go to bed I practice the Prayer, yet still I am not able to feel the difference," then take it for granted that something is wrong somewhere. Without exception, those people who say they have done everything and yet do not feel, have not done all that has to be done.

So all the suggestions, the processes, and the attitudes must be correctly done. Once we know the method correctly, the next thing is to fix the timing. Even when we only meditate for ten minutes, we can train ourselves to sit at that time every single day and then increase the duration. It is the vacuum that invokes Grace. And what is the vacuum in a seeker's heart? The vacuum is created by a deep craving and a feeling of centered-ness. Do we have that craving? Let Heartfulness be filled with passion, with fervor, and with a lot of love.

Make Good Use of Time

Let's return to the story of Babuji scratching a water canal on his hand and connect it to this idea of simplifying intentions. How can we remove unnecessary distractions from our lives so that we remain focused on the main purpose? There is another story about this:

In the days before the Mahabharata War, Guru Dronacharya wanted to find out how attentive his pupils were. He kept a toy bird on the branch of a tree and asked them all to take aim to shoot its left eye. Only Arjuna was able to shoot the bird exactly in the center of its left eye. Drona asked each one what they saw. They answered that they saw the tree or the branch or the leaves. Arjuna answered that he saw only the bird's head and then only its left eye. His single-minded attention helped him to become the best archer of his time.

Many people think they should wait to do meditation later in life, and focus on career, family, etc. while they are young. Some parents are even against their children meditating while they are studying or starting a career, because they think it will take them away from worldly activities. But let me assure you that meditation will help with career, family, and every other aspect of worldly living. My first meditation teacher was married very early in life, and her in-laws were very orthodox. Babuji had introduced her to meditation before she married, but after marriage her in-laws said, "You can't meditate in the house." Her husband was against it, so how could she do it? Everybody kept asking her, "What are you doing?" So instead of arguing with them, she would wake up early and do her Heartfulness Meditation under the blanket, pretending to sleep. In the evenings she would go to the toilet to do her Cleaning practice. She managed very well without causing any tension in her family.

When it comes to the spiritual journey, it is especially good to start young, when we have the strength and the stamina. When we are young we have time to read books, to acquire knowledge, to meditate, and to receive Transmission, Grace, and blessings from above. A time will come when the bodily pains of age get in the way. Even in bed we will not have peace, so how will we sit to meditate when we are worried about aches and pains? So it makes sense to achieve what we have to achieve now, instead of postponing it till later in life.

Once Chariji told me, "Make as much money as you like, but spend it wisely." Actually, when we spend wisely we don't need so much. In business, does it matter whether we expand operations from ten million to one hundred million dollars if the means we apply are honest and pure? No. There will be no regret and no guilt. We can also share our profits with others, and that opens up our heart. It is not that we make money only for our loved ones and ourselves. When we have the ability to give, we can explore it further.

If our efforts to make money for the sake of our material life are used to support our spiritual efforts, then the spiritual and the material wings of existence will fly together and become integrated. It is a matter of extending the wing of spirituality into material life. Then there is beauty in material proliferation.

Cultivate Humility and Simplicity

We have been exploring how purity weaves destiny, but we have not yet spoken too much about the impurities that can destroy destiny. Think about it: What kinds of moods destroy purity? Anger, hatred, doubt, temptation, fear, guilt, laziness, ego, jealousy, ignorance, judgment, and prejudice.

The first step is to identify our enemies so that we recognize them before they affect us too much. Now, how do we identify our friends? What are the good things that support purity and make it more intense? Love is number one, then patience, tolerance, acceptance, faith, discipline . . . we have a long list of friends.

In the Bhagavad Gita, Lord Krishna mentions the great qualities we must have in order to tackle the struggles of life. He uses an analogy: Life is like being protected inside a palace in which we live. Imagine that the palace is protected by a wall, with one noble quality protecting each gate of that wall. It is the back gate that is the most vulnerable in a palace, as nobody pays attention to it, and that is the gate of humility, which generally remains unseen because it is so small. It doesn't call for our attention. It is the place from which most enemies attack, the most unexpected place. Lord Krishna says that this gate must always be protected by humility. If we do not have humility, all the other gates are vulnerable.

In fact, if we have the qualities of humility and simplicity we can consider that we have everything; there is nothing more we need. With humility and heart, there is not only unspoken respect but also nobility. Nobility radiates when we walk or talk, and even when we are not doing anything. There is immense courtesy and civility in conversation. We strive for proper communication and go further into a state of communion: from communication to communion.

It is only when we break the wall of greatness and submit ourselves as humble and insignificant beings, subduing our behavioral complexities and ego, that life will be truly enjoyable. And for that we need to cultivate an attitude of surrender.

Now, who wants to surrender willingly? That is where the ego creates problems. But that is also where we can pamper the ego and make use of its qualities: "I will excel in this art of surrender." In this, the ego will help, and then we slowly say goodbye to it. Actually, there is nothing wrong in thinking ourselves to be great as long as we always think the other person is greater.

Be Natural and Truthful

Imagine for a moment the beautiful fragrance of a rose. Does the rose need to speak about radiating its fragrance? In a similar way, purity does not have to be spoken about, and love also does not have to be spoken about. Speaking about these things brings them down to a lower level. Qualities radiate naturally.

Yet often our intellect interferes, and we debate internally: "Should I do this or that?" When my inner nature is to emit purity and love all the time, where is the question of limiting myself by saying, "Okay, I should be doing just one thing at this particular time"? It is not natural. It is like those artificial perfume pumps that recognize your presence and emit a burst of fragrance when you pass by. Compare that to the rose.

Here is another simple analogy: Suppose we are on the riverbank relaxing. Suddenly a really silly idea comes: "Let's count how many waves are passing by." We then waste time doing that instead of relaxing and taking in the beauty of the surroundings, and as a result, we end up with a headache. Likewise, when we meditate, we can also try to be perfectly natural. There is no need to use any force to become thought-less or to try to recall the best meditation session that we had previously, or to think, "I *must* have the lightest condition!" We will only waste time. It is better to be natural, and then we can be immersed in purity. Otherwise, the condition we crave will be given only to satisfy our desire. It will not be natural. There is no need to presuppose anything in meditation or to meditate with the idea that we will be going deeper or to want the experience of a particular state. Be absolutely open. The moment we say, "I would like to feel like this," we are lost, because we are putting conditions.

Even in mundane human relationships, the moment we put conditions, we no longer have a relationship. For example, imagine saying to your boyfriend, "I will marry you only if you take me to the movies every week." What sort of a relationship is that? Why put conditions? So it is with God also. Why cheapen the relationship? With God there has to be no condition whatsoever. We just need to be ourselves.

It is often difficult to be completely truthful, even with loved ones, because we worry that they will not love us if we show them our true selves. If we remain artificial, however, we will never have proper relationships with family members and friends, because we will always be trying to impress or please them. There is no need to impress anyone. Whom are we fooling by doing so? Mostly ourselves. It requires a lot more effort to be unnatural. To tell a lie needs effort, because we have to remember it. To lie, we must be creative, whereas to speak the truth we need only be simple. The truth is pure, coming straight from the heart. Truthful people are content in their simplicity and purity. They are not trying to impress anyone, because they know who they are. They are what they are.

Speak with Love

During our wakeful hours, most of our time is spent communicating, and if we pay a little attention to how we speak we can greatly reduce the formation of impressions. I came across something very profound while studying the life and teachings of Lalaji—about how to address others and how to converse. It is one of the most valuable things I have discovered, and it has changed my life.

What does Lalaji say? Let the flow of conversation be a current that is even and in tune with the current of reality. In this way, you will touch the hearts of those listening.

How? Remove all sharpness so that your speech doesn't carry any kind of weight, like a current of still air. Let it be soft, cultured, smooth, and balanced. A person whose tongue is cultured and polite has a large, pure, and noble heart. Be free of anger and emotional outbursts in speech. The heart is so tender that it begins to wilt even with the slightest disturbance.

To develop such softness, be filled with such a feeling of love that you have no inclination to hurt anybody's heart, and then your words will not hurt anybody's heart.

The mistakes we commit during our daily activities arise mainly out of our conversations, because of what we should not have said and the way we spoke. Even the way we don't speak at times conveys a lot. We can transcend these shortcomings by keeping a continuous watch on ourselves and by connecting ourselves with the Source.

There is a humorous story about this. One day Mulla Nasruddin was asked to judge a dispute between two villagers. After listening to the prosecutor, he responded, "Yes, you are right."

The man was very happy and thought he had won the case: "You see," he exclaimed. "I told you so!"

After listening to the defendant, Nasruddin again responded, "Yes, you are right."

The local sheriff was baffled, and asked, "Your honor, how can they both be right?"

"You are right!" exclaimed Nasruddin.

Even in mundane relationships, it is differences that strengthen us—differences of opinion. You are able to see one perspective; your friend comes and sees another; your mother adds value to this new perspective; your driver might say something else. Through these various perspectives we understand things better. The trick is not to consider them as opposing opinions, or the people as your competitors just because they have different ideas. Different ideas broaden and expand our outlook, our consciousness, so it is much more productive to embrace them. Different ideas will always be there, at work, in the family, everywhere. That is what brings richness to life.

With emotional maturity we embrace diversity and learn to integrate all points of view.

There is one other aspect of communication I have learned from my Guides and found to be very beneficial, and that is to be very subtle and indirect. For example, say that you want to correct or criticize a certain habit in another person. Rather than speaking to them directly, it is often better to speak about it generally in a group, even sometimes looking at someone else entirely while speaking about that habit. That way the person can absorb the advice without becoming defensive or reactive.

Eat with Love

The second thing we all do during our waking hours is eat. Through conversation we imbibe and exchange thoughts and feelings; through food we imbibe and exchange energy and nutrients.

The state of mind we have while consuming food is very important. Earlier I mentioned how Dr. Pavlov trained dogs in his behavioral experiments during the 1890s. Pavlov also conducted an experiment with cats. He gave food to cats and measured the digestive juice secreted while they were eating. Then, one time, when the cats had just started eating, he brought in a dog. Seeing the dog, the cats were scared, and their gastric juice output was almost nil. So fear would not allow even a little bit of food to be properly digested. Similarly for us, if we are in a stressful or fearful situation, the vibrations that are negatively carried in the food also affect our bodies when we eat. And when the digested food goes to all the cells, it has a negative effect.

What happens at home when there is a quarrel at the dinner table? Will we digest our food well? When we meet at the dinner table, we often talk about family problems. There is nothing wrong with discussing family problems, but let's wait for a better moment. Let the moment of eating be like meditation, where we are so grateful to God for the food on our plates. When we consume food in such a state of mind, imagine the spiritual charge of that food! All kinds of spiritual diseases can be cured by this simple act.

There is no need to take my word for it. Observe for yourself. Compare what happens when you eat in a cheerful, grateful mood with what happens when you are stressed or disturbed. Now observe what happens when you are lost in remembrance of your inner Self and you eat with that inner state radiating its fragrance. Also, when you are preparing food, observe the effect of your mood. Be loving. It will have such a beautiful effect.

How to Accept Difficulties

What is the difference between coal and a diamond? Both are carbon. When coal comes under intense pressure and heat, it turns to diamond. Our existence is like that, too, yet often we don't want to go through the pressure of challenges, even though we know very well that the end result is always good. We talk so fondly of those difficult times: for example, "We walked all the way to the airport." We even boast about them. Would there be anything to boast about if we had gone in a car? When we really have a tough time and survive with integrity, we can say, "Wow, I did it!" Tough times really do make us stronger.

Challenges in life prepare us for greater things. We have an opportunity to learn from those moments. The best thing to do is to try to solve problems without getting frustrated, because when we get frustrated our minds are disturbed. When the radar is disturbed, there will not be guidance from within, and we will not be able to make the right decisions. So when challenges are there, we have to become extra alert. Instead of fighting them, invite them.

If we learn to accept miseries, we will understand their purpose and what they can do for us. To what level can they take us? All of these things will be lost the moment we avoid or react to struggles. If we go through difficulties peacefully, with a quiet heart, with a bold heart, and with a lot of courage, then we will emerge stronger. If we don't accept them, we will not learn anything. If we merely accept, we will remain mere human beings. To really transform our destiny, we need more than mere acceptance; we need to accept all situations joyfully and cheerfully and see the beauty that emerges.

This requires courage and self-confidence. If you do not feel confident in yourself, have confidence that your Guide will get you through this. Then you will come out a winner. Even if you fail in a worldly way, you will pass the exam of life with flying colors. If you face life as it comes and move on, with a smile, you will build your destiny. We all go through ordeals and difficulties—no one is an exception, but ordeals accepted cheerfully will bear spiritual fruits. In a way we can say that mastery is a life mastering many things: mastery of pain, mastery of pleasure, mastery of difficulties. Every situation is in our hands, and if we want to go further, we need to go beyond acceptance to cheerful acceptance.

And we can go even further, where we have no idea whether we have accepted with cheerfulness and gratitude; it really does not matter, as we have moved on. That is absolute acceptance, total surrender, and in that state of surrender we are always in the present. We are not anticipating anything different. We do not expect any change from the other.

When we go on anticipating better moments, we can never be happy. When we try to accept and make peace with the world, instead, and make peace with ourselves, then we have mastered our life. Then we will confidently, gracefully, walk through any situation in life without creating impressions, either in ourselves or in anyone else. Our existence does not create ripples anymore. If at all it has any effect, it sends out waves of purity and love.

In spirituality and in life, we are proceeding toward the unknown. So how can we have any expectations about the next step? We cannot. When expectations are dissolved, we accept things completely, and then our heart is content.

Poise

Have you ever had the opportunity to meet a great Guru or saint and observe his or her life? Perhaps you want to become like him or her. When we observe the lifestyles of such great beings, what appeals to us? What are the high, pristine qualities that stand out in their lives?

Let me share with you something about my second Guide, Chariji. There were so many outstanding qualities I observed in him, but the one that struck me most was his poise. He was never in a rush. Even when there were ten people waiting, he would attend to them one by one. When he would conduct group Meditation, he would take his time to finish it well. While giving an individual Meditation session, he would take his time. Whatever task was given to him, he would do it with absolute poise. When he cooked, there was love oozing in his movements. Even when he scolded us, there was poise and a lot of love. There was no element of rushing; he took his time in doing everything so nicely.

Mulla Nasruddin was said to have demonstrated this quality to his followers with his signature humor. One day he was seated on his donkey, rushing through the market-place. Followers and friends tried to hail him to chat every few meters, but he kept going faster and faster, replying, "I can't stop to talk now. Can't you see I am busy? I'm looking for my donkey!"

This captures the human predicament. It is critical to slow down; it is critical to have time for those around us and enjoy the beauties of life; it is critical to become conscious of the search and of ourselves as the seekers. So pause and try to remain poised, especially when everyone is rushing around you and there is pressure. Go into your heart, feel your Center, and recalibrate yourself. Try to approach the task at hand with poise and grace.

Sleep and Natural Rhythms

What are some of the natural cycles that we follow in our lives? To start with, we have a very regular pattern of breath-ing—inhalation, exhalation—which goes on and on. Another rhythm is that of our heartbeat. Then there is something that happens behind the breathing pattern at a deeper level—the inflow and outflow of energy—and, of course, there is the daily cycle of activity, rest, and sleep. Finally, we will explore how we can be more in tune with the monthly lunar cycle.

Only a healthy body can have a healthy mind and vice versa. A lot of people argue that a healthy mind makes for a healthy body, but without also having a healthy body, our mind will go crazy. "My legs are not working, my hands are not working, and so many other things are not working." We go to doctors and start worrying. How will we build our destiny when we have already chosen a destructive path, simply by not following the natural rhythms? So it is important to understand these rhythms and be in sync with them.

Breathing

Let's start with the subject of breathing. Just as each of us has a unique identity related to our iris and fingerprints, our breathing pattern is also unique to us. Not only do we inhale and exhale in a specific rhythmic way, when we examine our breathing further, we discover that our two nostrils also work differently according to the solar and lunar cycles. Take a moment to observe which of your nostrils is breathing more dominantly. Is it the left or the right? Or are they both the same?

In the yogic *shastras*, great significance is given to both nostrils. The right nostril is associated with the *Surya Nadi* or *Pingala,* and also with the sympathetic nervous system, signifying activity. The left nostril is associated with the *Chandra Nadi* or *Ida,* and the parasympathetic nervous system, signifying rest and repose. Every couple of hours the pattern can switch, but overall, there is also a very marked difference between day and night. Ideally, the right nostril is predominant during the daytime and the left nostril at night. If you check ten times during the day, you will probably find that eight times out of ten your right nostril is more active than your left, and the opposite happens at night. This physiology is directly related to the movement of both the sun and the moon.

When our balance is disturbed, a switch occurs. For example, what happens when we are angry? It is a sympathetic response, so the right nostril will be strongly activated and dominant. The same happens when we have a lot of fear and anxiety. During the sympathetic response, the hormones adrenaline, cortisol, and norepinephrine are released into the blood, so our heart beats faster and faster; our muscles tense, ready for action; our blood pressure goes up; and we become highly aware. We are ready for "fight or flight." In order to reverse this, we can use a simple breathing exercise.

Left Nostril Breathing

When you feel yourself getting angry, close your right nostril with your thumb and take a slow, deep breath through your left nostril, breathing deeply into your abdomen and releasing the breath fully each time. Then continue to breathe like this eight to ten times through your left nostril.

I invite you to try this for yourself, and if it helps you can share the knowledge with others. Normally, your heart will stop pounding, you will become calmer, and the emotional charge of anger, fear, or anxiety will dissipate to a large extent. That is because you have activated the parasympathetic system. But please also advise people who have an anxiety disorder to consult their physician.

3 Main Nadis

Sushumna Nadi
along the Spinal Cord

Right Nostril
Pingala (पिंगला)

Left Nostril
Ida (इडा)

Sun Current
Surya Nadi

Moon Current
Chandra Nadi

In the olden days, when people could not sleep they would get up and examine their breathing. If their breathing was not as it should be, they would drink hot water, do *Pranayama*, walk, etc. When we observe our breathing very carefully just around sunrise, we witness a slow shift from left to right, and at sunset a slow shift from right to left. And when we meditate at one of those transition times, it will be wonderful. It is just the right time, because the balance is there between your Surya and Chandra Nadis.

As an experiment, observe yourself at night and during the daytime at random intervals. Is your energy pattern one of absorbing or radiating? At the time of observing your energy inflow or outflow, also observe whether you are breathing through your left or right nostril. You will be able to find a relationship between the inflow and outflow and your breathing pattern. We can all contribute to this research.

Daily Rhythms and Hormones

Early in the morning, before dawn, nature's energy flows in one direction toward the Source. This is not a physical energy but something much subtler. It is best when we flow with those currents, and this happens when we meditate before dawn. It is wiser to meditate just before sunrise, because very naturally Transmission flows with your natural inflow of cosmic energy at that time. After sunrise, energy is naturally flowing outward, so it is not as easy to absorb Transmission. It also makes sense to do the evening Cleaning at a time when the energy flow is outward, as we are throwing things out from our system. This happens when the Surya Nadi is active, for example, just before sunset.

Our genetic predisposition is geared toward responding to these solar cycles and other natural cycles, based on millions of years of evolution.

During the daytime we are predisposed to a certain pattern of breathing and level of activity. Since time immemorial, our forefathers developed a natural routine of life based on these cycles. Most activities were performed during the daytime, and nighttime was for rest. So the body acquired a rhythm of activity and rest, day and night.

To be in tune with these cycles, our forefathers generally rose early and greeted the sun. For example, in Hatha Yoga we have the *Surya Namaskar*, the sun salutation, which was often done in the early morning, outside, facing the rising sun. And still today, in some villages in India, you can see people in the early mornings practicing the traditional Hindu ritual of offering water to the sun. Scientists now know that sunlight activates nerve pathways from the retina of the eye to the hypothalamus, which then leads to serotonin production. Serotonin is our "happy" hormone, and without it we are prone to depression. Being out in the sunlight in the early morning kick-starts our serotonin production for the day, giving us that bright, joyful feeling toward life. Sunlight on water also releases negative ions into the atmosphere, vitalizing our system even more. There is great scientific wisdom in many of the ancient rituals!

Not only that, enough serotonin is a prerequisite for the production of another hormone in our bodies called melatonin. Within the pineal gland, serotonin is chemically transformed to yield melatonin. Melatonin levels start increasing in our bodies about two hours before we are programmed to go to sleep, so if we are sensitive enough to feel this natural rhythm we will start to wind down for the day in a restful mood, and then eventually prepare for the night. If, on the other hand, we continue watching TV or playing video games late into the night while our bodies are trying to prepare for sleep, it is like swimming against the current.

This daily hormonal rhythm is an integral rhythm, where one thing leads to another: rising early and being out in the sun leads to serotonin production, which leads to melatonin production, which allows us to sleep well, which allows us to wake up early again the next morning. When this cycle is disturbed, we are prone to sleep problems and depression, two of the most significant maladies of the modern world.

Sleep for Well-Being

This brings us to the importance of sleep. Disciplining our sleep cycle changes our life. How well we sleep and how deeply we sleep determines our state of mind throughout the day. Generally, it is better to sleep early to be in tune with natural cycles. Also, our morning Meditation will improve drastically, as we are not struggling with our consciousness. When we meditate with a well rested mind, we have a good grip over consciousness, whereas when our consciousness is crippled because of lack of sleep, will it be easy to wake up for morning Meditation with a fresh mind?

When we are fully alert in the morning, lovingly we can invite the higher consciousness and be one with that essence. Then some beautiful conditions will be created in the heart. And when they are so intense, they stay glued to us, whether we try to hold on to them or not. If we try to shake them off, they will not go away. Such is the influence or the permanency of the condition created when our consciousness is ready to receive. If our morning Meditation is hampered, as it happens after a bad night's sleep, the whole day is affected. For someone who has never meditated, or who meditates every now and then, it makes very little difference. It is just another day gone. We can compare that level of consciousness to roaring oceans. They look so dramatic and poems are written about them, but real beauty is when there is a still pond without any waves and there is utter serenity all around.

So the choice is ours. If we choose to lead a life like the roaring ocean, we will be lost in the waves of our disturbed consciousness. Per contra, when our consciousness is still and settled, even the slightest change or variation is noticed, the way the fall of the lightest leaf on a still pool of water creates ripples. They are felt. So sleep matters.

If we get the right amount of sleep, the right nostril will automatically be active in the morning. Over millennia our systems have evolved in such a way that when the sun rises, certain hormonal patterns are triggered. When we are in tune with that rhythm, our health automatically improves.

What happens to people who go to bed very late at night? When we go against the rhythm, again we are swimming against the current, and our decline in health over time will speak volumes. It is better to set a healthy pattern as early as possible in life. Nightly activities are one of the curses of the modern world. Because of electricity, there is now not much difference between the day and the night. Starved sleep patterns result from irregular habits and late nights, and health suffers as a result. Immunity levels also go down because our nervous system is under stress.

Extensive studies have been conducted on people who work at night, and it has been discovered that, among other things, they age rapidly. Unlike those who have to do shift work for their livelihood, most of us do not have to work at night. We have a choice, yet we choose to stay awake late at night, watching all kinds of things. Whether we look at it for spiritual growth or health, if we go to sleep early, it will help us a lot. Remember the wisdom of the old English proverb, "Early to bed and early to rise makes a man healthy, wealthy, and wise."

There is an enlightening TED talk by Jeff Illif called "One More Reason to Have a Good Night's Sleep," in which he describes how our neurological system detoxifies itself during sleep. Our central nervous system does not have any lymphatic drainage, so the cerebrospinal fluid flows through the space between the cells removing toxins from the brain, and this happens during sleep. In a person whose sleep pattern is normal, this drainage of cerebrospinal fluid is effectively able to remove the toxins, but in sleep-deprived individuals the toxin removal is reduced greatly. These toxins then affect us, so we become vulnerable to bad moods. When we are sleep-deprived, what happens in the morning? We are cranky. We become irritated. So it is not surprising that sleep-deprived individuals are responsible for a large number of road accidents. They also cannot engage themselves in creative discussions and fruitful conversations. They become irritated with every little difference of opinion.

Here are some tips for getting a good night's sleep:

- Rise early in the morning and spend a few minutes out in the sun.
- Around sunset, or when you finish your day's work, do the Heartfulness Cleaning so that you are able to let go of the worries and stresses of the day.
- Wind down in the evening for a couple of hours before sleeping, so your brainwaves slow down and you are able to naturally transition into sleep.
- At bedtime, first analyze what you could have done better during the day and let go of any wrongs you have done, vowing not to repeat them. Then do the Heartfulness Prayer so you sleep in a deeply open relaxed state, connected to your Center.

If you still have trouble sleeping, try the following:

- Wash your feet before going to bed.
- Try sleeping on your right side, as it activates the parasympathetic nervous system, helping you calm down.
- Imagine gentle, cool water falling from above your head, calming you.
- Drink a glass of warm milk.
- Do the Heartfulness Relaxation lying down in bed.
- Listen to relaxing music. Some music that is particularly good for sleeping can be found at www.heartfulness.org/en/good-night-sleep.

When we want to excel in life, we will find a way to naturalize our sleep patterns. Otherwise we struggle with that one fundamental thing all our lives. We have neither the proper consciousness for everyday activities nor a proper spiritual condition. We uproot our consciousness, the very guiding force, and so we leave ourselves vulnerable to greater emotionality and reactivity. More and more, we collect impressions throughout the day. Then our ability to remove those impressions through Cleaning suffers, so Meditation suffers, and it becomes a vicious cycle.

If instead we have a fine condition, a pure condition, a blissful condition, we will feel lightness and gratitude. This gratitude emerging from the heart creates a bond between God and us. There is great benefit in it, and as we receive more and more benefit, we feel like doing more and more.

Lunar Cycles and Fasting

Our bodies are composed of 60 to 70 percent water, so the moon has a significant effect on our being. Just as you see the impact of the gravitational pull of the moon on the water in the oceans—the tidal range is over fifty feet in some places—similarly, the moon has an impact on the water in our bodies, and the "Lunar Effect" has been observed in many other species of plants and animals.

The term "lunatic" actually comes from the lunar effect on the human system, and especially during the full moon, records show that criminal activity is greater than usual. The ancients in India must have observed this, because they noted that from the 8th day of the lunar cycle, the effect of the gravitational pull of the moon starts increasing and reaches its peak on the 14th day. Midway between these two is the 11th day, which they called *Ekadashi*, which is Sanskrit for the number 11. There are two Ekadashi days in each month: one in the first half of the month when the moon is waxing, and the second when the moon is waning. These days have a special significance for health, and many people fast on these days. The practice was also connected with religion so that people followed this ritual for their health and well-being. Our forefathers discovered that when we moderate our intake of food on the Ekadashi days, we moderate the gravitational impact of the moon on our system.

The concept of fasting to balance the system also ties in with the fascinating work done by Dr. Yoshinori Ohsumi on autophagy, for which he was awarded the Nobel Prize for Medicine in 2016. Autophagy is our body's internal recycling program and is the process by which the body consumes and recycles its own damaged cells and unused proteins. This happens more effectively when we fast. After an infection, autophagy eliminates those cells that have been infected by bacteria and viruses. Interestingly, in many traditions there is the saying, "Starve a cold." I believe our ancients observed these correlations across the physical, emotional, and mental spectrum, and thus started the ritual of fasting on certain days. So a sensible hypothesis is that autophagy has a role to play in our emotional and mental well-being, beyond just the physical benefits, and more research needs to be done to verify this.

One of the most important principles in life is to be in tune with nature. We can swim with the river's flow, or we can swim against the flow—but what do we get by resisting?

Radiation

Electromagnetic technology is an integral part of most of our lives. Manmade sources of electromagnetic radiation in our environment include Wi-Fi, Internet, Bluetooth, mobile phones, computers, tablets, microwave ovens, and medical equipment. Today we are starting to learn more about its long-term effects. In May 2011, WHO's International Agency for Research on Cancer announced it was classifying electromagnetic fields as "possibly carcinogenic to humans" and advised everyone to adopt safety measures to reduce exposure.

There is now a field of research known as bioelectromagnetics. Authorities in Sweden, Austria, Germany, and France, among other countries, recommend their citizens do the following:

• Use hands-free electronic devices to decrease radiation to the head
• Keep the mobile phone away from the body
• Do not use a phone in a car without an external antenna.

How do electromagnetic fields (EMFs) affect our biology and health? Our subtle body is our energetic body, which has its own electromagnetic field created by the negative and positive polarity of charge. As a result, the subtle body is affected by other energy fields in the environment—for example, the buildup of positive ions in the atmosphere before a thunderstorm creates restlessness, while the release of negative ions once the storm arrives brings relief.

In nature, everything is in a state of dynamic balance or equilibrium, with complementary energy flows switching just like alternating currents throughout any given day. The same sort of alternating pattern is seen in the complementary sympathetic and parasympathetic currents associated with the Surya and Chandra Nadis, where at times one predominates, then the current switches so that the other predominates. Then there are the main inflection points at sunrise and sunset, the stationary points, where the turn of the flow is more prominent, like the turning of the tide. We see these patterns of polarity at the macrocosmic and microcosmic levels, whether in the planetary movements or in particles at the atomic movement.

What happens when we add man-made EMFs to the environment? They interact with our natural EMFs. So the stronger the wireless technologies in our city environments, the more they are likely to affect us. Some people are sensitive, and get headaches, rashes, nausea, and nervous complaints. The evidence is still inconclusive on whether EMFs cause these symptoms, but the effects will happen first at the level of the subtle body, the energy field, and will eventually filter down to have a physical effect. In fact, most diseases start in the subtle body as an imbalance or disturbance, which is why Traditional Chinese Medicine works on the meridians and Ayurveda on the *nadis* and chakras. Just because we don't measure a physical effect, it does not mean that nothing is happening at more subtle levels.

A few years back, a group of girls in Denmark did an experiment at school. One of them said, "We all think we have experienced difficulty concentrating in school. And if we had slept with the phone next to our head, we sometimes also experienced difficulty sleeping." They took 400 watercress seeds and placed them in twelve trays: six in a room without radiation, and six in the next room with two Wi-Fi routers. The seeds were given the same amount of water and the same conditions of light. After twelve days the cress seeds next to the router did not grow so well, and some of them mutated and died.

The experiment drew international attention, and scientists replicated it with double-blind controls and other experimental variables, such as using other plants. Here is an example using mung bean seeds in seed trays in four different environments. Try it for yourself and see what happens.

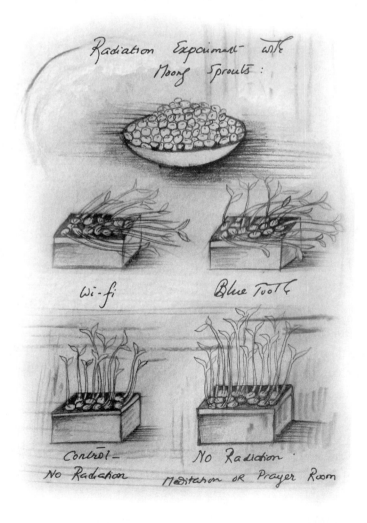

One of the Danish students said after finishing their experiment, "None of us sleep with our phones next to our beds anymore. Either the phone is put far away, or it is put in another room. And the computer is always off."

Here are a few simple things that will also make a difference:

- Turn off the Wi-Fi when it is not in use, including at night.

- Use a mobile phone in the car only when necessary, and don't charge the phone in the car.

- Keep your mobile phone in a bag, not in a pocket on your body.

- Switch Bluetooth on only when needed.

- Keep your phone away from the bed when you sleep.

- Avoid giving small children phones to play with like toys.

These technologies have brought us many benefits, not the least of which is the fact that people across the globe can connect so easily, families can stay in touch, and businesses can thrive. They have revolutionized our global network. But they have significant downsides, and today many of us are dependent on these technologies to the point of addiction. The radiation accompanying these devices may well be harmful to health because of its effect on our subtle body, our consciousness, and only time will tell the long-term effects of constant use.

Today we look back at the Romans and wonder why they were so foolish as to use lead utensils for cooking, resulting in lead poisoning. Will the people of the 23rd century look back at us with the same incredulity for our rampant and unregulated use of these digital technologies?

CHAPTER 10

TRANSFORM YOUR RELATIONSHIPS

I F YOU ASK most people in their twenties today about what is on their mind, they will say relationships and career. It may also be the same if you ask people in their thirties and forties. Relationships matter because we live in families, communities, cities, and nations. By nature we are social creatures, and conflict in any of our important relationships can tear us apart. Yet how many of us can say that we know how to nurture healthy, happy, positive relationships? Here are just a few of the things I have learned over the years about relationships.

Respect

Mutual trust and respect is a fine quality to have in relationships, but often we are more concerned with self-respect, expecting others to respect us rather than making an effort to respect them. I do not have a lot of respect for self-respect, as it is usually childish, and not really helpful for our growth. But let's consider a higher approach toward the subject. Here is what two of the Guides of our Heartfulness tradition have had to say about self-respect:

Babuji: "Self-respect, as I understand it, means that one should not do unto others as one would not like others to do unto oneself."

Lalaji: "Everyone should remain reserved with one another. One should not give opportunity for too much talking— that is, do not give a long rope for discussion. One should not reveal one's household secrets to all and sundry. One should not consider oneself as weak. One should not utter anything that may drive others to become unmannerly toward you. All of this constitutes the definition of self-respect."

Now let's concern ourselves with respect for others. It is actually the epitome of love for yourself. If you do not love yourself, this very fine quality can never develop inside you.

Take a situation where you felt angry because you did something that made you unhappy with yourself. Can you respect others at that time? It is not possible. Now contrast that with how you behave when you are in a state of love. Even when an enemy comes before you, because of the way you behave, he will feel, "Look! He is treating me so well." He then goes back changed.

Respect for others is expressed in many ways. If you were invited to visit a dignitary, for example, would you wear shorts? No, because you want to show respect to the person. The principle here is not that we want to look good, but that we want to make an extra effort when visiting someone of a certain stature. When we wear a tie to the office because guests are visiting, we do it as a mark of respect for them. It is not that we want to show off. It is precisely to show respect toward others that we dress in a certain fashion.

Similarly, the way we speak, the way we sit, and the way we hold our head conveys something to the people we are meeting. When we slouch in front of guests, it is not respectful. Though we may not speak a word, our behavior says it all. When we express ourselves without sincerity or feeling, our looks and manner convey it.

Some people walk into a room as if they have created a storm, banging doors and stirring up an agitation. The way they walk, talk, and look around speaks volumes. They carry an atmosphere of disrespect, because they do not have love for others. They do not have respect for others.

Also, what about our relationships with children? We often take children for granted and fool around with them, thinking they are unimportant. Compare this with Babuji's relationships with little children. He would say "*Aap*," meaning "Thou," because he had so much respect for the young ones.

I have seen that when we address a child with a lot of respect, we invoke the same quality in that little fellow who is trying to come up in this world and grow. But if we keep telling him, "You stupid fellow, sit down, you should not be doing that, behave yourself," all the time lecturing and joking and putting him in a corner, he will learn to behave in the same way. Thus, from a very early age, the idea of respect is foreign to him. If children do not know what respect is, it is because elders do not respect them.

So when a small child has an idea, like, "Oh, this flower is beautiful," praise her by saying, "Yes! It is such a wonderful flower; you are right." Guide her to do more research. "How many petals are there? What is the color? How do you like its fragrance?" Help her develop her analytical abilities. When we start from scratch, we will see where it can go.

Love

I would like to explore the topic of love, starting with a scientific concept. What is entropy? Let's understand it with a practical example. Say you bring a book home from the library, your father gives you another book as a gift, your girlfriend gives you magazines, and you have a collection of music CDs. They all pile up on a small table in your room, so now there is clutter. The rest of your room is also in a disorganized state: your clothes are scattered on the floor, your socks are under the bed, and your towel is hanging on a chair. This is a disintegrated system, and it is chaotic.

Eventually you become frustrated with the mess and clean everything up. You put each book on the shelf where it belongs, wash your laundry, and make your bed. Now the room looks clean, until again you start scattering more books and other stuff, and again the system disintegrates. To keep things in order requires constant energy input.

Entropy is the degree of disorder or randomness in any system. The second law of thermodynamics says that entropy increases over time. It reflects the instability of a system over a period of time if there is no energy input to keep it stable.

Our human relationships can also become unstable because of the disorder that develops from the interactions we have day after day. We let things build up inside. We store more and more emotions and reactions, creating inner disorganization, just like the books and clothes in the bedroom. We harbor resentments and irritation, until one day we explode—unless we do something about it. We need inputs to stabilize relationships and iron out the wrinkles or differences so that we do not harbor and store things forever in our minds.

What is the input that is required? Is it that we have to give constant external input to keep our relationships stable? Do we have to offer ice cream and candy to pacify the other person every time we make a mistake? This would mean constant investment to maintain a relationship. When constant input is required every time there is a fight or an argument, it will require greater input each time. At the same time, it is our business to love each other, whatever the cost. We may get hurt in the process, and there will be a lot of energy invested from our side, but if we are prepared for it, the relationship will improve.

How does this play out in daily life? In a family, if we have to tolerate each other it means that constant input is required, and that is not ideal. In fact, it means that it is not a loving family, even though we may be together. Contrast that with a family where there is love and acceptance among all, where we do not have to offer ice cream or a paradise vacation to patch things up, where it is taken for granted that we accept each other with love. So it is the love we have in our hearts that is the input that stabilizes relationships. With love there is a greater level of acceptance. By acceptance I don't mean tolerance. Tolerance may be a virtue, but when we have to tolerate someone's mistakes, we do not have that level of acceptance that comes with love. Love irons out everything. And where does love come from? It comes from a pure heart, from a genuine heart. Distrust kills relationships, whereas when there is love, acceptance, and purity, sacrifice is natural and we are able to let go of everything.

So this principle of entropy helps us to understand the importance of love in relationships. When the constant state of our being is love, then the need for inputs disappears: zero input is needed. When zero input is needed, it means that it is the most stable relationship, the most stable family. There is no need to explain anything, because where there is love there is no need for explanations.

In the case of true love, what happens? Love begins, and the hearts of both people expand. You accommodate anything and everything about one another. Even the mistakes of the other are so adorable, and you do not fight. Then the next stage comes. When you really start loving, you start losing yourself. You start merging with the other person, and you want to do everything to make the other person happy. You don't worry about yourself at that time.

So why do love marriages fail? It happens when the reciprocation is not equal. The degree now starts varying, and you start judging and thinking, "I should not have done this." You start retracting because you do not want to lose yourself completely. You are afraid, and that fear arises out of the ego. You have now started remembering yourself, and the relationship goes haywire. You become aware of your own needs, whereas earlier you were not aware of them. You wanted to do anything and everything for the other person. Now you start realizing, "What has happened to me? I was a great doctor, but now I am sacrificing so much." And then the relationship fails. The moment the idea of "I have sacrificed" arises, it is the end of the love story.

So should we not think about ourselves at all when we are in love? Of course we still need to focus on our own continuous improvement even when we are in love. This is just a cautionary tale: if you find yourself resenting the other person, or noticing how much you are sacrificing for the other, then know that your ego is raising its head and you need to take note. Our personal continuous improvement, on the other hand, is not egotistical in nature, but is a gradual process of rising above self-centered responses, having less concern with personal desires, and becoming more accepting. It actually helps us to be in a state of love and resonance with others. If you reflect on this in relation to your daily actions and thoughts, it will become clear.

Acceptance

Many young people ask me, "What is the most important factor in choosing a life partner?"

I can only say, "Use your heart. And from whatever I have seen so far, the little of life I have lived, I would say do not expect too much."

Life is all about acceptance. And when we learn the art of accepting whatever comes, whether it is a situation, a business outcome, or a partner, it is the acceptance that makes it successful. Even bacteria mutate to survive in a hostile atmosphere, so why can't we? We have to learn to constantly adapt to situations without being so disturbed. There is no perfect human being. We are colliding against each other with our imperfections. If we are seeking perfection, we have to question ourselves first: Am I perfect?

Many people want to know if horoscopes are important in determining the right partner. Perhaps the best way to answer this question is to share the example of Lord Rama from the Ramayana. All the rishis checked, double checked, and triple checked the horoscopes at the time of his marriage to Sita, yet Rama had to struggle for fourteen years with his wife, making her go through difficult tests. She had to endure an ordeal of fire after her abduction by the demon king Ravana. What sort of a husband was he?

Sita boldly suffered everything. As Swami Vivekananda put it, there has been no woman like Sita on this planet and there shall never be. Even the most chaste, pure woman was questioned, not by an ordinary man but by a divine incarnation. So it is better not to expect too much. When we are able to accept what life throws at us, we can move on happily. Even the most perfect match can be disastrous, because we do not know what previous samskaras will surface when, and what new samskaras are forming now.

Our responses to life are very complex, and they become all the more obvious when we ask ourselves two questions: "How well do we accept our own faults?" and "How well do we accept the faults of others and the circumstances around us?" It is worth pondering over our responses deeply, because if we keep accepting everything, what is the point in continuous improvement toward perfection? "I accept my imperfections. I am so happy and I am at peace. I don't have to change." Is that sort of acceptance useful?

You probably know the joke where the husband comes home rushing to his wife and says, "Papa and Mummy are coming this evening." He gives this news to her with so much joy, but his wife starts grumbling, "Not again! Why do they keep coming so often?" The husband just keeps quiet. Then, in the evening, the doorbell rings, and she sees her own parents standing outside! She is so happy. What happened to acceptance there?

We accept certain situations with so much joy and have aversion to others. It is when our hearts become small that acceptance bids goodbye. We easily accept people and their idiosyncrasies when they are our own. When they are not our own, it is a different matter. But spirituality says something else. So please think about it. Whenever any situation in your family, your business or your work environment demands a certain level of acceptance, see how far you can go. Keep thinking.

If acceptance is done out of habit, or is enforced, then we are performing another ritual in a refined way. For example, "I must accept this, otherwise I am going against the philosophy of Heartfulness" is not a useful thought, especially if the heart says otherwise. We need to accept situations in life with full alertness and full awareness. There is no point blindly saying that we have to accept something because someone else says so. Then it will not be true acceptance.

I would like to share with you a personal story about acceptance. It happened after Babuji's passing on April 19, 1983. Sometime on the 18th, while I was working in a pharmacy in New York, I felt as if my whole body was deflating. The energy was just leaving me. So I told my boss that I needed to go home, as I couldn't work anymore that day.

In the middle of the night I got a call from a family friend in South Africa with the news, "Boy, our Babuji is gone." Two days later, I took a flight to Shahjahanpur and, by the time I reached there, he had been cremated. Nevertheless, I had the opportunity to collect his holy ashes, put them in an urn, and keep it in his cottage.

At that time Chariji was announced as Babuji's successor, but in my heart I felt, "How can anyone succeed such a great personality?" I promised myself, "I cannot let Chariji live peacefully; I will act."

So with this attitude I hired an Ambassador car and, along with three others, set off for Fatehgarh, where I wanted to pay my respect to Lalaji and take an oath that, come what may, I would not let Chariji succeed.

On the way, just as we were discussing all of this most vehemently, for no rhyme or reason our car toppled sideways and fell into a ditch. Fortunately it was a dry ditch and the local villagers turned the vehicle back upright and lifted it onto the road again. But it was not drivable, so we took a bus back to Shahjahanpur. This gave me a jolt: "There must be something wrong in your thinking. Hold your horses! Don't be too emotionally carried away. Start praying."

So I started praying to Babuji, and dream after dream led me to the realization that Chariji was his successor. But the dreams only started appearing the moment I became neutral, when I was neither against nor in favor of the decision. I think that this is the prerequisite for taking the next step: we neither accept nor do we not accept. I had come to a neutral midpoint.

I think that this is a good first step in any such situation; only when we come to a midpoint is there the possibility of a solution. If I had remained adamant in my belief that nobody could replace Babuji, I would have lost. By coming to the midpoint there was the possibility of higher forces working upon me so that I was guided correctly.

So the number one step in acceptance is letting go of the possibility that this is so or that is not so, in order to come to a neutral midpoint. Whenever you want guidance from nature or from God or from your Guide, allow yourself to come to that neutral point and then see how you are steered in the right direction.

When we come to neutrality, it is as if a burden is lifted. Whether in family life or in business, before making a final decision, come to a neutral point and see whether you should accept or reject whatever it is. When we arrive at neutrality, we let go of our prejudices and preconceptions. Prejudices make our decisions one-sided, whereas when we are neutral, we are able to see with a clear vision. With neutrality, confidence is emboldened. When the direction is right, the heart feels lighter.

There are two questions about acceptance that are really worth reflecting upon:

1. What is the difference between expectation and hope?
2. How can we balance acceptance and responsibility? In other words, when does acceptance become irresponsible?

Collective Destiny

My young associates are quite idealistic and passionate about social change. They often ask if we should be contributing more to nation building and social causes, instead of focusing so much on self-development. But suppose we want to change the entire population of New York City and we have the ability to do so, but *we* do not change. How will that work? Generosity begins at home, with ourselves, by equipping ourselves so we can help others. We need a million dollars in order to give someone else a few hundred thousand. If we do not have money, but we are still hoping to give someone a million dollars, it is a pompous act. We will rob one person to give it to another.

Similarly, when we do not have peace of mind, how can we offer peace to others? There are some teachers who create a disturbance the moment they enter a classroom, and there are others who inspire us and we just want to be around them. There are also certain friends whose association you like because of the person they are.

We are moving toward perfection. Perfection in what? Not in our outer appearance or other external matters. It is the perfection in our inner balance, our inner flawless character and manners. In 1957, Babuji addressed a letter to the United Nations on how to bring about world peace, highlighting a method to uplift the entire universe. He suggested that everyone sit daily at a fixed hour with the thought that "All people of the world are growing peace loving and pious." Our state of balance, our inner condition, has an effect beyond the immediate environment as we progress. Its impact is galactic in scale.

So what can we do to change the world? First, at the very least, let's not make the world any worse. When we do our own practice of Cleaning, we are not only removing impressions for our own sake, but we are contributing to the harmony of the home, of the neighborhood, and eventually, of our whole network. Many of us have had the experience that when we wake up early and complete meditation, our children wake up happy and smiling, whereas the day we skip meditation, our children are affected. Our meditation has a definite and immediate impact, changing the vibratory level of the surroundings, and innocent children are very sensitive to these changes. When they are used to "good" vibrations, they miss them when they are not there.

Think about the impact of thoughts on the atmosphere around us. What is the atmosphere like in a jail? That atmosphere is created by the collective thought patterns of the inmates. What is the atmosphere like in a hospital? That atmosphere develops because of the state of mind and consciousness of all the patients and their loved ones. Any collective thought-form or vibration created by a group is called an egregore. The egregore in a church, a temple, or a meditation hall is one of piety, unless of course people are thinking about their problems and worries instead of meditating or praying. Every place has a different vibration, and we create that atmosphere through our collective thought patterns.

Say you are happy, for example, and you try to represent that feeling of happiness on a graph, it will be like a wave pattern. If you come together with another person who is also happy, the wave pattern they create will likely join with yours and have a potentiating effect. As many happy wave patterns come together, the curve will only heighten. This is how an egregore forms, of similar feelings and thought patterns.

Normally we are not aware of how we actively create an egregore, as it happens without us even having to try, simply due to the collective thought energy we create. That is how we change the outside environment. It happens automatically. Wherever the rose goes, the fragrance goes. Wherever we go, whatever we carry goes with us. If I am foolish, my foolishness will go with me. If I am a joker, my joking habit will follow me around and people will laugh at me. That is the impact of the traits that we carry with us on the external environment.

So imagine what we can do if together we purify our consciousness so as to contribute to an enlightened egregore! We are all connected intellectually, morally, and spiritually. Even criminals are so well connected it would surprise you. The black marketeer in Assam knows how much tea he has to stock in the warehouse, and when he releases that information to somebody in South India or to somebody in Dubai, they do a deal. They are connected for profit. The members of terrorist organizations are also well connected. The mafia members respect each other so much they share data: "I got a contract with this labor union. You go to this department and finalize the deal. That is your part."

So what about spiritual people? Are we so well connected and supportive of each other? It does not really require active input from our side. We just have to let things happen without interfering in the process. This connection will automatically happen once we start purifying ourselves. We will then feel that what we create within ourselves merges with the collective feeling, and we will become a part of the entire scheme of things.

That is why Babuji invited us to help raise the vibration of the egregore. How? By purifying ourselves through practice. When we do this, we become ready for the transformation that will bring change to humanity, and that will also be passed on to the next generation. It is the vibratory level that is preparing this change. The extent to which we have purified ourselves is the extent to which we will contribute to the future course of humanity. So our inner preparation has a great effect, a great echo into the future. The egregore that we prepare, the field that we prepare, has its impact. By meditating regularly and well, wherever we are, together or alone, the impact will be felt beyond our immediate environment, and will benefit all of humanity.

Our power is no less than Godly power, because at the very root of our mind that original stir that happened at the time of creation still continues to work. For example, when Lord Krishna approached Duryodhana just before the beginning of the Mahabharata War, he tried to convince him not to go ahead with his plans to wage war. And Duryodhana told him, "Look, Krishna, I know who you are. I know your abilities. I know I may lose also in the process. I know what is good." He continued, "I know what is my duty, I know what I have to do, but I cannot compel myself to act in that direction. I also know what I must not do, yet I cannot stay away from it."

Sometimes we are like Duryodhana. We know what is right, but often we convince ourselves that we are helpless: "I cannot do this. I know it is right, but I cannot," or "I know what I must not do, yet I end up doing it." Even when we pray to a Guide who has the great capacity for Transmission, it does not work. Why? Because we prevent it. Our thought force is so powerful that even the great Guides fail in their efforts to change us. Nobody can be changed unwillingly. We must participate in this process of change willingly and joyfully. Deep down, we need to know, do we really want it? We must have the desire for it.

PART III

DESTINY, FREE WILL, AND FREEDOM OF CHOICE

*So far we have explored the Heartfulness practices
and the lifestyle that goes hand in hand with these practices.
In this final section, we will explore how these create our destiny.
The philosophy is too broad to be explained in just one chapter
of the book, so this is only an overview. Many of the concepts
will be explored in more detail in later books.*

CHAPTER 11

DESTINY

BABUJI GAVE A beautiful message to some of his associates in 1982.[2] In fact, it inspired this book.

> We are all brethren connected intellectually, morally and spiritually—the main goal of human life. This and that have gone now. There remains the purity alone in all His work and environment which weaves the spiritual destiny of the Being with the Ultimate.

He gives us an inkling of the goal of life: our spiritual connection. "This and that" refers to duality, to the opposites of material existence—good and bad, right and wrong, dark and light, etc. So we eventually go beyond the opposites; we transcend the dualities of worldly existence when we cross the Heart Region and enter the Mind Region, where purity starts dawning more often.

In his books, Babuji described three broad regions of the mind: the Heart Region, the Mind Region, and the Central

---

2. Ram Chandra, *Complete Works of Ram Chandra*, vol. 3. (India: Shri Ram Chandra Mission, 2009.)

Region.[3] Within the Mind Region there are also five main regions—the Cosmic Region, the Supra-Cosmic Region, the Region of Surrender, the Region of Transition Between Surrender and Oneness, and the Region of Oneness with God. So in total there are seven regions. To describe each of these properly would take longer than is possible in the scope of this book, so here let's just say that the Heart Region covers the sphere of our material existence and consciousness in the physical world. The Mind Region is the realm of potentiality that supports consciousness, the state before things are manifested in the physical world. The Central Region is the realm of "Nothingness" or vacuum that exists at the center of every atom and also at the center of our own existence, which supports our whole existence. Think of matter versus energy versus space from physics and it will give an idea of these three states of being. Matter is the heaviest, energy is lighter, and space is the subtlest of the three.

The description of these regions is a whole philosophy in itself, which you can read about in Babuji's book, *Efficacy of Raja Yoga*[4]. But for our purposes here, in the light of destiny, it is important to know that as human beings, we are made up of all three regions. Also, we have the potential to realize all of them. Our destiny is by no means only tied to the physical plane of existence; in fact, it is very much dependent on all three regions, and our Heartfulness practices are designed to take us on the journey across all three realms.

---

3. Ram Chandra, *Complete Works of Ram Chandra*, vol. 1. (India: Shri Ram Chandra Mission, 2015.)

4. Ram Chandra, *Efficacy of Raja Yoga in the Light of Sahaj Marg*. (India: Shri Ram Chandra Mission, 2014.)

7 Regions:

A — Heart Region

B — Brahmand Mandal, cosmic region

C — Par-Brahmand Mandal, Pare-cosmic Region.

D — Prapanna, Region of Surrender

E — Prapanna-Prabhu, Region of Oscillation

F — Prabhu, Region of Oneness with God.

G — Central Region.

When we evolve through a spiritual practice, we continue to live in the physical world until our time is up, but we also develop our capacities in the other two regions or realms of our existence. Because we nurture our subtle and causal bodies, we are able to soar into dimensions other than the physical realm—into the cosmic realm and beyond.

Here is a simple experiment: take a glass cup or measuring cylinder and fill it up with dirty water. Let the dirt slowly settle, and as time passes, you will see how the densest material goes to the bottom and purer water remains on top, except for some floating objects. Likewise, the samskaric "dirt" is mostly to be found in the Heart Region, because impressions are formed in our physical existence. When we expand beyond the limits of this physical realm, we find more and more purity.

As we soar higher, traveling through expanded, refined consciousness, we experience more and more of that purity that weaves our destiny with the Ultimate. At a human level, our aim is to establish this connection. When we do establish it, we get a taste of Divinity and start to mold our lifestyle so as to match the finer levels of subtlety, as we have discussed at length in the section on Lifestyle in this book. Through this process we weave our destiny with the Ultimate.

What is this destiny with the Ultimate? It is not just our destiny in the physical world in which we live our daily lives. In the worldly sense, we want a good life: a happy family, a beautiful house, adequate material goods, a successful career, and making a useful contribution to humanity. All of those things are important, but they relate to our growth in this physical world, and they cannot come with us after we die, to the hereafter, to any other dimension. In order to have a fulfilling destiny with the Ultimate, we also have to pay attention to developing those inner qualities that prepare us for our journey into the hereafter, because our causal and subtle bodies continue on to other dimensions after we leave this physical body. That preparation cannot happen only in old age or at the moment of death; it is built up gradually throughout a lifetime, in parallel with worldly existence.

Babuji used a beautiful word in his message: "weaving." Weaving creates a fabric from separate strands. He is speaking about the joining together of different elements, and in the terminology of many spiritual traditions and religions this is known as "mergence," or *laya avastha*. This is another way of describing the osmosis mentioned earlier in the book.

Our higher spiritual destiny has everything to do with the purification of the subtle body. We do this by removing the layers of impressions that surround it so it can merge with the Source (described in the chapter on Heartfulness Cleaning in the Practice section). These layers form a covering that can be compared to a coating of oil on water. If a water droplet is coated with oil, it cannot merge with the ocean, because water and oil do not mix. That oil-coated droplet of water will float on the ocean's surface for millennia. We may remember God all our lives, but if this oil coating of samskaras remains, we will never merge with the Ultimate. That is the reason why we go on removing layer after layer of samskaras in order to reach the destination.

13 chakras

SDK
Sakasra Dal Kamal

11
SDK
10

Top of the Head

11
12
13

Back of the Head

CHAPTER 12

THE MEANING OF
EXPERIENCES

THIS JOURNEY THROUGH the Heart Region, the Mind Region, and the Central Region takes us across thirteen points, or chakras:

- to deeper and deeper levels within the heart,
- across the full spectrum of consciousness,
- and beyond consciousness to potentiality to absolute nothingness.

The simplest way to try to understand "consciousness, potentiality and nothingness" is to relate them to "body, mind, and soul." Consciousness is associated with our physical existence, the Heart Region; potentiality is associated with the Mind Region; and nothingness is associated with the causal body, the soul, the Central Region. Consciousness arises out of potentiality, and potentiality arises out of nothingness. God is omnipresent, so exists in all three, although the Absolute nothingness is the ultimate realm of God.

In reality this journey never ends, and each point is an infinite universe in itself. This can be known by experience. The first point, the second point, and so on up to the thirteenth, are all infinite in their expansion. We could continue meditating on the first point of the heart infinitely, life after life after life—that would be horizontal growth. In our spiritual journey, another kind of growth is involved, which we call vertical growth.

After some expansion at the first point, we move to the second. There again, there is infinity. We can easily be lost in the infinite potential of the second point, but a Guide of caliber pushes us to the next level, the third point. It goes on and on like this until we reach the thirteenth point.

Once a person asked Babuji, "Can you show me God, or, at least, tell me what God is all about, this original state?"

Chariji was with Babuji at the time and he thought, "This old man may be caught out today! What will he answer?"

Babuji said, "Suppose I showed you God, how would you know it was God?"

So the question is: *How do you experience it?*

Remain open to whatever you receive.

How do you keep yourself open?

Do thorough Cleaning and expand your consciousness to receive Transmission.

What can you do in order to receive Transmission?

The best way is to meditate so that you prepare yourself little by little, and in the process you will experience inner states and conditions.

By experiencing these things you will also become something. It is not enough just to have experiences; you must also change and become something—and this is the process of designing your destiny.

Suppose we didn't ever experience anything in Heartfulness. Would any of us keep meditating? Probably not. Does that mean that these experiences are just carrots, given to us only so that we continue? No. Experiences have another purpose. If we were to experience the entirety of spirituality or infinity in one go, none of us would survive till the next moment. It would be like going to the gym and being asked to lift a 1,000 kg —could you do it? Suppose somebody helps you to lift 1,000 kg but then leaves you holding the weights. That is what would happen to us if the Guide became so generous as to give us such an electrifying experience all in one go. We would be finished.

So instead we start building up with a 5-kg weight, a 10-kg weight and then a 15-kg weight. Slowly, we start enduring the physical stress. In the same way, we start facing the ultimate peace within, experience by experience.

You might have observed that some meditators go straight into a sleep-like absorbed state of Samadhi when meditating, and they may even start snoring. It indicates a weak consciousness in some way. You must have heard of drug users who are gone with the first dose, knocked out all night, but after some time they take five doses, still stand on their feet, and even attend classes or the office. I have seen it in my pharmacy practice. There is a drug called diazepam, which is a sleeping pill. If you take 2.5 mg, you will not be able to stand up; you will go to sleep. But I knew a pharmacist who would take a 20-mg tablet and still work. He was addicted to it, and his system was used to it.

It is similar with these doses of purity, sanctity, simplicity, and divinity—we don't need to become highly evolved beings overnight. We want to expand our consciousness slowly.

Step-by-step we cross the great distance so that we are able to adjust to each new environment as we journey on.

At the beginning we have many experiences. We are impressed by the lightness we feel during meditation sessions with a Heartfulness trainer, because we are experiencing such profound things and it is so amazing. Even if we do not feel anything during a meditation, the aftereffect takes us by surprise as the experience unfolds. In fact, often we will feel more afterward than during a session, as the meditative state is absorbed throughout our system. Later on, as we progress more and more, we still have experiences, but they are of a different nature. They are spiritual in nature, so they are not so dramatic and impressive. As we go higher, there will be fewer and fewer experiences, and when we reach the Central Region, there will be no experience. It is so super fine and without qualities; it is like a desert wasteland.

Upon reaching that state, Babuji complained to Lalaji, "What to do now? My earlier days were a lot better. This feels like nothing. I don't find any enjoyment with this condition."

So Lalaji asked him, "Should I remove this condition, since you don't like it?"

Babuji said, "No, my Lord, please don't do such a thing. If you do that, this will be my last breath. I won't be able to survive."

Although there is no beauty or attraction, it is such a state that you cannot exist anymore without it. That is what we are aiming for: the purification of consciousness to its highest state.

CHAPTER 13

EVOLUTION

EVOLUTION IS MY favorite topic. It is actually a much bigger topic than most people imagine, when we include the three bodies of a human being—the physical, subtle, and causal bodies. What do we really understand by evolution? If you ask around, most people will say that evolution is all about change. But what evolves in human evolution, and how are destiny and evolution intertwined?

Let's start with what is familiar. We learned about biological evolution at school: all the theories about morphological change, cellular change, and genetic change. It is only due to more recent research in epigenetics that scientists are starting to accept that our thoughts and emotions have their own effect on genetic adaptation and evolution.

For example, one of the pioneers in the field of epigenetics, Dr. Bruce Lipton, explains in *The Biology of Belief* what happens when a baby is conceived in a broken family where there are constant fights and discord, and the mother-to-be is always under stress. What is the physiological response to any sort of violence, whether physical or psychological? It is the fight-or-flight response. If somebody tries to attack her, she will either fight back or run away from the scene so she doesn't have to fight. Either way she needs strength. Under both circumstances she needs her limbs, so blood circulates to the limbs and away from the visceral organs like the stomach, liver, spleen, lungs, and brain. When the mother is always under stress, the blood flow is more often toward the limbs, and the same happens with the fetus that is growing within, so the blood flow to the fetus's limbs will be greater than to the visceral organs. The limbs of the child will be longer than in normal human beings.

The second thing that happens is a difference in the growth of the posterior and frontal lobes of the brain. The frontal lobe for cognition and the intuitive faculties develop when the fetus gets a chance to grow in a healthy family environment where there is love and affection. Where there is stress and tension, the back part of the brain grows bigger because the blood flow goes there more often.

The father's brain may be well developed and his limbs normal, and the same may be true for the mother, but the fetus will have longer limbs and an underdeveloped digestive system. The subtle bodies of the parents, others who come in contact with the baby, and the environment in which the baby is developing have a definite effect on how the baby's genetic pattern will manifest itself.

Because meditation purifies and refines our subtle bodies, it can play a very important role in epigenetics. When we meditate, what happens? Scientists have done experiments on people who have meditated for 10,000 to 20,000 hours. The myelin sheath that surrounds and insulates the nerve fibers, or axons, becomes thicker. Also, the frontal lobes of the brain are well developed in people who meditate regularly and for reasonable periods of time. So meditation itself has a definite evolutionary effect even on our physiological system. But that is not our goal here. Despite all of these good things, our real evolutionary goal is beyond all these physiological changes.

Most of us are afraid of change, even though we want our lives to change for the better. The problem is that change creates so much discomfort that it shakes our foundation. Take the case of a husband and wife sharing a bed where they have each slept on their own side for years; let's say the wife is on the right side. Now if one day one of them requests a change, there will be a fight. Even such a simple mundane change becomes a challenge! So when something as massive as our inner spiritual atmosphere changes, we rebel, because our comfort zone is totally shattered. We are used to certain feelings and a certain inner environment.

We have thirteen major points, or chakras, from the heart onward, all the way to the Central Region. One way to describe our spiritual evolution is as a journey from one chakra to the next to the next and, finally, to the thirteenth chakra. We travel through an inner universe that is infinitely vast, with each chakra like a different galaxy in that universe.

And as we move from one galaxy to the next, there will always be a reaction to the movement and the change it brings. In his book, *Towards Infinity*[5], Babuji describes this process of entering each new chakra. He describes the heaviness that develops in the mind, the unsettledness. For many of us, it becomes very difficult to meditate when we feel the discomfort that results from being in a new galaxy.

5. Ram Chandra, *Towards Infinity*. (India: Shri Ram Chandra Mission, 2020.)

So how can we best navigate this? Ask for help. On the days when you don't feel like meditating because your mind is heavy, when you are not in the mood, ask a trainer for a meditation session or use the HeartsApp on your phone to have a session with a trainer. It helps to adjust to the change more easily. Because you are on an evolutionary path, you will find a way to navigate this and adjust to the change.

Each movement, from one chakra to the next, brings with it a new atmosphere inside, as the inner canvas of our consciousness changes so much. As a result, we become unsettled in our practice. But if we wait for these moments with anticipation, we can congratulate ourselves on our progress.

I will share with you an experience. A young lady from Germany came to visit one of our ashrams in India after she started meditating, and she was praising Heartfulness to the skies. I said, "Hold your horses," and presented her with a diary. I asked her to write what she was saying on the first page, and then I told her that those who have experienced the three introductory Heartfulness sessions generally acknowledge that this is the best thing that has happened to them, yet many drop the practice after some time. She asked for an explanation.

So I responded, "This euphoric feeling that you have is not going to last. Soon a new stage will come when you will move to the next spiritual chakra, and you will say, "Where am I? Why am I here? This does not feel so good anymore." But that will pass, and after a little while you will know that you have progressed and your consciousness has expanded. It is just the change that feels uncomfortable. So please read this first page and remind yourself that this is the best thing that has happened to you. Read it again when you go through every new phase."

After some time she wrote to me, "I am not feeling so bad at all. When am I going to progress?"

When we understand the mechanics of spiritual evolution, we learn to welcome the discomfort that comes as an indicator of growth, and the inevitable turbulence that accompanies it, in the same way that an athlete welcomes the discomfort that comes with the training necessary to move to the next level of performance. Also, think of the sort of turbulence that can happen in a flight or in a ship. When such turbulence comes in spirituality, it also means we are moving, whereas if we are steady in our comfort zone, it means we are not moving, and it becomes the Guide's job to help us move and evolve. When we resist change, he will not push us. Instead he will create circumstances so that we start craving more and more. The Guide is always there to accelerate this process of evolution, but our dynamic and active participation is also needed. The wise among us value time!

Just imagine what is possible if we cooperate, happily accepting the bumpy patches of the journey, and desiring higher and higher conditions. And there are also many more positive changes on the journey. There will be discomfort when we first move to a new chakra, but when we settle down there we will feel at home and we will start to feel so good. The experience of bliss at each successive chakra becomes more and more beautiful, consciousness keeps expanding to new levels, and the clarity and subtlety of the state keeps improving.

The Guide keeps us moving. Once the good things have matured in us at each successive chakra, once we have mastered the field of feelings and experiences at that particular chakra, he creates the conditions so that we gently move to the next chakra. If, of our own accord, we start asking, "Please, I would like to go further," we will willingly trigger new conditions from our side. That is the key to faster evolution: not being afraid of change but welcoming it.

The Three Bodies: Body, Mind, and Soul

In order to understand this better, let's explore more deeply the three bodies of a human being: the physical, mental, and spiritual bodies. The first is our physical body, made of flesh and blood. Movement of the sense organs and of perception is the characteristic of the physical body, and action is the nature of this body. While it changes according to how we live our lives, it doesn't change much. For example we can become fitter, but we cannot become one foot taller or develop extra limbs. Physical evolution happens over longer periods than one lifetime, so we don't expect our physical body to evolve much in this life.

We also have the mental body, also known as the astral body, the subtle body, the vibrational body, and the mind. It is the field of the heart and mind and is associated with energy. It has the characteristic of thinking, feeling, and understanding. This is the realm of thoughts, feelings and emotions, intuition, inspiration, ego, intellect, wisdom, courage, love, and consciousness. There is both movement and rest in it.

The third body is the spiritual body, also known as the causal body—the cause of our existence—and the soul. The causal body is associated with the absolute state of "nothingness"; it is the base of our existence. Peace or rest is the quality of the soul, which contains all movement in seed form. This causal body is ultimately pure, unchangeable, and immutable, and its evolution is not something we can work on directly. It evolves as a natural outcome of our inner journey through the chakras.

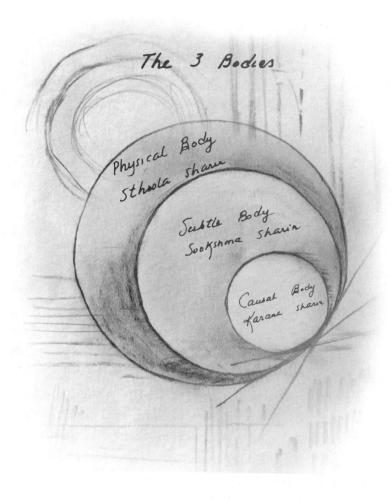

The body where our transformation happens, through which we evolve, is the middle of the three bodies, the subtle body. Remember that our species is Homo sapiens, and our raison d'être is the mind, knowledge, and wisdom, so that is where our evolution happens. Our destiny has everything to do with the evolution and purification of the subtle body.

This evolution happens when we remove the layers of complexities and impurities so as to purify and awaken all the chakras in our system, and then we find that consciousness evolves. This is how we design our destiny. This is what our Heartfulness practices are for.

These three bodies are common to all life. You can understand this by equating them to the concept of the three states of matter, energy, and absolute space in Physics—states that exist in everything in the universe.

In the Mineral Kingdom, all three bodies are so closely tied together that it is difficult to separate them; they don't have much freedom. To the extent to which they have different vibrations, they have different qualities, and so we give them names like gold, lead, osmium, and so on.

In the Plant Kingdom, the three bodies are less tightly bound together than in minerals. When we observe plants, we see that they have subtle bodies that respond to stimuli. Have you seen flowers that open up as the sun rises and close again when it gets dark, like hibiscuses, Californian poppies, lotuses, and magnolias? Heliotropic flowers turn to face the sun as it moves, such as sunflowers, poppies, marigolds, and daisies. There are also plants like *Mimosa pudica* (lajwanti, or "sensitive plant"), with sensitive leaves that fold inward when you touch them. When there is a breeze, or even a storm, the leaves and branches of trees dance, but the moment someone tries to cut off a branch, a tree will become agitated. Modern researchers[6] describe how trees communicate through their roots, with the help of fungal networks. They also describe the language of trees, how trees build communities and help each other in forests, and how trees learn. Even with all of this, however, the subtle bodies and the causal body of plants are more tightly bound together than in animals.

Animals have still greater separation among all the three bodies than plants do. In human beings the three bodies have the potential to be even more loosely connected, but this also depends on each individual and his or her qualities. Some people have the three bodies tightly bound together, while others show extreme plasticity and freedom. There is a gradient of separation. You might have heard of the three *gunas,* or qualities, in Vedic philosophy: *tamasic, rajasic,* and *sattvik.* These three qualities reflect how loosely or how strongly the bodies are connected in human beings.

A tamasic person is more like a stone or mineral, where the bodies are more tightly bound together, and so the subtle body is not so free. As a result, consciousness is restricted. Such a person will appear to have a very limited mental capacity, not always grasping what is happening around them. Even when we explain something, they won't always understand, because the subtle body is just not free enough to grasp the concept.

In a rajasic person, the subtle body has a lot more movement, but consciousness is restless and disturbed. The mind is fickle, being pulled in many directions by pleasures and desires. As a result, consciousness is more chaotic and cannot expand to its full extent.

---

6. D.G. Haskell, *The Songs of Trees.* (Australia: Black Inc., 2017.)

A sattvik person has an expansive, pure consciousness. The subtle body can move around easily so that the sattvik person can project their thoughts anywhere. There is lightness in thought, flexibility, and a sense of wonder toward everything around.

Generally we are a mixture of these gunas, according to our purity and qualities. It is along the gradient of flexibility of the subtle body that we choose to evolve, expanding our field of consciousness.

It may appear that our existence is based on the physical body, and upon this base the subtle bodies and the soul sit, but the reality is the opposite. The soul gives birth to consciousness; actually, they are inseparable. Consciousness then creates its own identity, the ego, for its existence. The ego then uses the intellect for its existence. And for the intellect to thrive, it needs the thinking function of the mind. So in fact it is the soul that supports consciousness, which in turn supports ego, which in turn supports intellect, which in turn supports thinking, and these support the existence of the physical body.

The Subtle Body

The subtle body is our energy field. We can think of it as the field of the heart and mind. It can either be turbulent and complex, like a roaring ocean during a storm, or, at the other end of the spectrum, it can be like a still pond where even a feather landing on the surface creates a ripple. This is where Heartfulness practices have a vital role to play, as they give us the tools to purify and simplify this field, bringing clarity, stillness, and peace.

The heart is the field of action of the mind. What does this mean? There are four main functions within this field—consciousness (*chit*), thinking and feeling (*manas*), intellect and wisdom (*buddhi*), and ego and identity (*ahankar*). They exist together to make up what we know as the mind, and we call them the four main subtle bodies or elements of the subtle body.

Actually, nineteen elements of the subtle body were described by the Gujarati saint, Haridasji (1862–1938), and they are:

- The five cognitive senses: sight, hearing, smell, taste, and touch.
- The five conative senses: our main energetic processes of elimination, reproduction, movement, grasping with our hands, and speaking.
- The five pranas, or energy flows, known as the *vayus*: the inward flow, the downward and outward flow, the integrating balancing flow, the ascending flow, and the circulatory flow.
- The four *antakarans,* or inner functions of the mind: chit, manas, buddhi, and ahankar.

It is the four antakarans that we primarily work with for our evolution. The other fifteen elements also become refined and balanced through the yogic practices of Heartfulness. Of these four, it is consciousness, or chit, that expands and evolves to weave our destiny, but this happens because of the refinement of the other three. Consciousness is like a canvas to a painter, and on that canvas the play of the other three bodies is orchestrated daily. You could say that they have their existence in consciousness.

Chet -
Consciousness
to
Divine
Consciousness

Buddhi -
Intellect
is Wisdom

Manas -
Thinking
is Feeling

Centered
in the
HEART

Ahamkar -
Ego is Love

The Four Subtle Bodies

We are actively expanding our consciousness so that it evolves. Our spiritual practice creates conditions for progressively stilling the mind to deeper and deeper levels, thus allowing this expansion. At a physical level, we exercise to strengthen our body's muscles. For the mind to evolve, for consciousness to expand, we need to exercise what belongs to the subtle level of existence—manas, buddhi, and ahankar—to free consciousness so that it can expand and soar. This is done through meditative practices.

Meditation and the Meditative State

What does meditation have to do with this? We meditate to exercise and regulate the mind. An unregulated mind is pulled by wishes and desires, fears and habits, in many different directions. It is rajasic in nature, and it becomes weak as it scatters energy in too many channels. Remember the water canal that Babuji drew on his hand? Compare this to a regulated mind with focus: one application, one channel. When we meditate well, we regulate our minds so that our consciousness can expand and evolve.

Our thinking, intellect, and ego are all refined and developed through meditation. We simplify our thinking process from many channels to one channel so that we learn to concentrate through the practice of meditation. Then we go deeper, from thinking to feeling. Feeling gives us greater direct perception, greater intuition and ability to work with our emotions so that we refine our lifestyle and integrate external behavior with inner states.

We learn the art of observing and witnessing the play of our thoughts through meditation. This helps us to work with our emotions and reactions, especially when the ego is creating problems. We become more sensitive and alert.

Holding and nurturing the meditative state throughout the day is another outcome of good meditation, and helps us to balance and deepen the mind even more. When we are in this state of constant awareness or remembrance of the inner state, our canvas of consciousness cannot be spoiled. It remains fresh and clean, and is not sullied by the formation of impressions.

The subtle bodies span the full spectrum of consciousness, including the subconscious, conscious, and superconscious aspects of the mind. Swami Vivekananda once said, "Consciousness is a mere film between two oceans, the subconscious and the superconscious." We can also imagine subconsciousness as being a vast ocean, consciousness as the surface of the land, and superconsciousness as the sky going out into the universe. As we evolve, our consciousness expands along the full spectrum, opening up the vastness of our human potential. Another way of saying this is that we go deeper and deeper into ourselves, from our starting point on the surface.

Scientists say the same thing in another way. For example, in *The Biology of Belief,* Dr. Bruce Lipton says,

> When it comes to sheer neurological processing abilities, the subconscious mind is more than a million times more powerful than the conscious mind. If the desires of the conscious mind conflict with the programs of the subconscious mind, which "mind" do you think will win out? . . . the greatest problem that we face is that we think we are running our lives with the wishes, desires and aspirations created by our conscious mind. When we struggle or fail to obtain our goals, we are generally led to conclude that we are victims

of outside forces preventing us from reaching our destination. However, neuroscience has now established that the conscious mind runs the show, at best, only about 5 percent of the time. It turns out that the programs acquired by the subconscious mind shape 95 percent or more of our life experiences (Szegedy-Maszak 2005).[7]

Dr. Lipton does not mention the superconscious, but Arthur Koestler published a book in 1964 called *The Act of Creation* on how superconscious inspiration manifests in human creativity. When we ponder over great scientific discoveries and yogic findings, the source of such discovery and inspiration comes from the superconscious, which is able to blossom when a person is in an overall relaxed state. Consider the great discovery of the Archimedes Principle, or the fundamental principle of gravitation by Sir Isaac Newton, or radioactivity by Madame Curie, or the discovery of the structure of the benzene molecule and the double helix structure of DNA. They did not appear as a result of rational deductive thought, but instead emerged through dreams or when their discoverers were completely relaxed and not "thinking." Spiritual findings and scientific findings share the same source. They are not opposed in their approach. But even without acknowledging the superconscious, Dr. Lipton does point out just how much vaster the subconscious is than the conscious mind. With the support of Transmission, we are able to expand our consciousness in both directions, to explore these previously unknown territories of the subconscious and superconscious.

---

7. Bruce Lipton, *The Biology of Belief.* (Carlsbad, CA: Hay House, 2008.).

SPECTRUM OF CONSCIOUSNESS

SOURCE

Purpose

Subconscious

Superconscious

Available thin film

of consciousness

Intellect, Prayer, and Cleaning

In the process of diving deeper within, intelligence becomes more and more heart-based. Intuition and inspiration develop as consciousness expands along the spectrum, and buddhi is fine-tuned, like a sensitive antenna picking up the signals of the heart. As a result, the intellect expands to include more and more wisdom. Often we think of a wise person as someone who makes wise choices, but with this process we go much further into a different dimension altogether, where choice is no longer required, because the heart's wisdom is so pure and correct. As a result, emotional intelligence, social intelligence, and spiritual intelligence all blossom naturally.

There is a big difference between an intellectual person and a wise person, and the practice of prayer also helps us to move from mere intellect to wisdom. Prayer takes us into the heart, connecting us to the Source, where we are able to let go of any mistakes we have made, deciding not to make the same ones again. Is this not wisdom? If we succumb to foolish mistakes day after day, hour after hour, we are not becoming wiser. We become wiser when we wish to change from the bottom of our hearts and ask for help to do so. When we live with this attitude every moment, wisdom flourishes.

Wisdom means to utilize to the best of all our faculties. Wisdom is to have the maximum output with the minimum input. With minimum action we have the maximum result: more and more with less and less effort. Only with a meditative mind, only through meditative acts in our day-to-day life can we expect to have such good results.

For this to happen, the subtle bodies have to be pure; otherwise it is like expecting to see the bottom of a lake through muddy, turbulent water. There is no clarity in a turbulent mind. The practice of Cleaning past impressions is therefore necessary for consciousness to evolve.

Ego

The third subtle body is the ego, ahankar. The ego plays a vital role in whether or not the expansion of consciousness occurs. The ego is often seen as the bad guy, but it is essential for life and for evolution. It is an active function of the mind—the doing, thinking function—and we need it in every aspect of daily life, even to want to evolve. It gives us our identity. It is the activating or initiating force. If it is used wisely, it serves us well, but when the ego is used for selfish purposes, we become arrogant and self-important. When we constantly refine the ego, consciousness develops very rapidly.

What does "refine the ego" mean? The more humility we have, the more beneficial the ego is for our evolution. All great teachers of spirituality, religion, and ethics have given so much importance to this aspect of character formation. They have valued the quality of humility so highly that at any cost it must be maintained. The philosophy here is that there is nothing wrong in thinking ourselves to be great, as long as we always think that the other person is greater.

Otherwise the ego can be like a black hole. It can have a very strong gravitational pull upon our consciousness, preventing consciousness from expanding. Just as the earth's gravitational pull does not allow us to fall off the earth into infinite space, likewise our ego can bind consciousness and restrict it to a very limited field. This happens to an extreme extent in a very narcissistic person, whose consciousness contracts in on itself and can become stonelike. Another example is a very arrogant man with a bloated ego. Have you observed how such an individual communicates with others? In contrast, as we become more and more humble, consciousness is able to expand infinitely, and goodness is expressed through cultured communication.

The ego manifests itself in many ways. For example, a concert flautist performs, giving so much joy to the listeners and they reciprocate accordingly. Now, as an artist, he will not be happy unless he surpasses his previous performances. It is the ego that makes him perform well. In this way, the ego can help us to develop excellence in any field, worldly or spiritual, through self-respect and self-pride. It can be our best friend in helping us outperform our own past performance. But to think that no one can play the flute better than us is not a welcome manifestation of ego. It is blatant ego at its worst, known as arrogance.

The ego raises its head in all sorts of daily situations. For example, when we are having a discussion at home with our children or spouse, there are times when there is a disagreement. Generally, when the other person is unable to accept our point of view, we label them egotistic. So we relate nonacceptance with the ego: the person is unable to accept because of ego. And in today's world, individual freedom is given so much importance that there is no possibility of oneness. If individuality is at the cost of others, then it becomes a source of conflict and separation. In a state of perfect oneness, there is no hurt arising out of ego—and selfishness dissolves.

Imagine two or three individuals, each with their own strong ideas, having a discussion. Though they may all be very intelligent, their beliefs and ideas will separate them and they will not come together. But the moment we respect the ideas and opinions of others and honor them, then the various differences that we all have can be integrated together, which will only enrich our thought and broaden our perspective. We can only respect and harness each other's talents, opinions, and ideas when the ego is subdued. When there are multiple egos involved in any situation, it can lead to a clash of egos in that "multiverse." There is a possibility of unity when we admire one another in a true sense, in an authentic way. So we can say that acceptance is an antidote to the ego.

Think about it: Is the ego involved in the state of acceptance when we say yes to someone else's request? Not at all. But when, instead, we fight it out, or we say, "I reject that," then the ego sounds quite magnificent—so big and so heavy. When we say "Yes," many possibilities automatically open up. When we say "No," it's a dead end. When we accept, the ego dissolves—and when the ego dissolves, there is transcendence.

Thinking and Contemplation

The fourth function of the subtle body is *manas,* which is the function of thinking and contemplation. During Heartfulness Meditation, the first step is to bring the attention of the mind from many scattered thoughts to just a single thought, the source of divine light in the heart. We practice being one-pointed, and over time, concentration develops naturally. But it is not necessary that throughout Meditation we stay stuck on this one thought. The thought should leave at some point so that the object of thought can be *felt* in the heart.

If we keep thinking during Meditation, we will have a headache, and consciousness will not expand. The initial thought, the object of Meditation, is just a springboard to take us deeper. It is an assumption, or hypothesis, as in a scientific experiment. This assumption is eventually proven to be correct when we start to dissolve in the experience of the presence of the divine light upon which we are meditating. And then we go deeper and further—as we feel that presence, we slowly disappear so that even that feeling is gone. Then the ego is gone, and we are not even there to experience it.

As *manas* evolves through Meditation practice, thinking evolves and expands to encompass feeling, and eventually expands beyond feeling to the state of being, then to the state of nonbeing, to merge into the absolute state of existence. Once again, these states only make sense through experience.

Consciousness

As intellect, ego, and thinking evolve through our spiritual practice, these subtle bodies become lighter, purer, simpler, and more refined, and the lake of consciousness becomes still with almost no ripples. It can expand and evolve.

Now, what can we do with this expanded consciousness? We can do much more than simply enjoying it during Meditation. Let's say we have a particular state after Meditation and are aware that the condition we have received is good. Then we go off to work. We have already discussed how to hold that condition throughout the day. More than that, why not also radiate that condition willfully, consciously, and with the confidence that wherever we go it will spread its fragrance?

After Meditation in the morning, think for a while that, "The condition that is within me is also outside me. Everything around me is absorbed in a similar state. When I look at people or talk to them or listen to them or am silent, I let that condition spread everywhere." Let consciousness expand wherever it finds its way.

When we observe the subtle bodies of highly evolved beings, they have complete freedom. The subtle body can travel anywhere, do any spiritual work that is given, and return back. That is why in spirituality we have the tradition of the living Guide. However great the past saints and spiritual teachers may have been, they cannot directly help us in the same way that a living Guide can. Why is this so? Because the spiritual work requires our psychological mindset to be corrected, and the living Guide is able to use his subtle bodies to remove the samskaras of the seeker at the root through subtle suggestion, cleaning, Transmission, and prayer.

Many a time I witnessed Chariji reading letters or meeting people who wanted to explain something in words to him. Without any words being spoken, he felt what was needed. There was no thinking involved in the process of making a decision. He was able to give very wise advice to help people without having to think things through, because his *manas* was so evolved. Another example of this comes from the anecdotes of Swami Vivekananda about Ramakrishna Paramahansa, when he said, "I could not believe my own ears when I heard Western people talking so much of consciousness! Consciousness? What does consciousness matter! Why, it is nothing compared with the unfathomable depths of the subconscious and the heights of the superconscious! In this I could never be misled, for had I not seen Ramakrishna Paramahamsa gather in ten minutes, from a man's subconscious mind, the whole of his past, and determine from that his future and his powers?"

Levels of Subtlety

With spiritual progress, we become lighter and lighter, so we slowly adjust to greater subtlety in everything we do, including daily activities like the food we eat. It is also because of the greater freedom with which the three bodies are connected in an evolved human being that it is beneficial to eat lighter, vegetarian food. As mentioned earlier, the physical and subtle bodies of plants are generally more closely bound together than in animals, and the more evolved the animal, the greater that separation can be. The less tight the tethering of the subtle bodies is to the physical body, the more possibility of pain there is in death.

Imagine that a great saint is in front of you. It would be unthinkable to eat that person because their subtle bodies are everywhere. He or she is one of the most evolved beings in the universe, and if you were to kill them the pain associated would be enormous because of their highly evolved consciousness. The subtler the being, the more evolved the subtle body, so the more pain there is. And that pain is then transmitted to whomever or whatever consumes it. The vibratory level of the food we consume becomes a part of us.

How do we adjust to increasing levels of subtlety? When you finish your Meditation, try to hold that state even though you have to struggle with all the incompatible things around you. It is a challenge, and that is where our exercise begins. The subtle body has to adjust—consciousness, thinking, intellect, and ego all have to adjust to the surroundings. That is why, in the beginning, we get so angry if something disturbs our peace during meditation or after we have finished. After some time we get used to these disturbances, and we master the art of holding on to the meditative state no matter what is going on around us.

To what extent can consciousness develop? When consciousness, thinking and feeling mind, intellect, and ego reach their highest potential, consciousness is able to evolve to the level of divine consciousness. At the pinnacle of evolution the mind is completely open, with no fear. Such highly evolved souls are totally free, totally open.

So this whole exercise is about the evolutionary process of reaching our highest potential of consciousness. Another way of describing this journey is that we are going back to our original consciousness, our original state. Now, in that original state we had no samskaras, we were completely pure and light. So what was the first samskara that came into being when we were first created? It was fear, the fear of separation from our Source. Once that first samskara of fear is removed, the rest of the samskaras are able to leave on their own if we remain open to change. And in Heartfulness, that foundation of the samskaric edifice, primordial fear, is removed in the first few introductory Meditation sessions.

During the introductory Heartfulness Meditation sessions, three gifts are given:

1. The ability to effectively practice your own daily Cleaning is enabled.
2. The Divine Light already existing in your heart is ignited.
3. The connection between your heart and the heart of the Guide is established.

The art of living is to live without demanding anything, being grateful to the Ultimate. This itself is a big step in evolution: accepting what we are, what others are, and moving on. We have enough difficulty changing ourselves, so why try to change the world? Even God cannot change the world, which is His creation. So why break our heads trying to change our spouse, our children, our boss? Cheerful acceptance is a quantum leap in itself.

The four fundamental elements of the subtle body—consciousness, mind, intellect, and ego—are dynamic principles. They express themselves in our day-to-day behavior and interactions. Our behavioral patterns are actually a reflection of the level of purity of our subtle body expressed in the simplicity and purity of our lifestyle and relationships.

In the Heartfulness practice of Cleaning, what is the suggestion that we make? That all complexities and impurities are going away from the back. See how simple it is? When complexities are gone, we become simple; when impurities are gone, we become pure. It is a beautiful method, a flawless method, with the suggestion every evening that all complexities and impurities are going away. That fundamental thing, the removal of complexities and impurities, is a powerful process.

CHAPTER 14

DESTINY AND VIBRATION

Vibratory Compatibility

COMPATIBILITY IS AN extremely fine concept. When compatibility is not there, where is harmony and unity? Things don't gel. For example, when an IT professional from a poor Indian background goes to work in a European city for a big company, sometimes he will be put up in a five-star hotel without knowing how to use a knife and fork or a bathtub. He will be out of sync with that environment until he adjusts his lifestyle to match the surroundings. He is not yet compatible with the environment. Or take another example: when you take one medication, and by accident you eat something that is not compatible with that drug, there is a war inside you and you suffer as a result of it.

Compatibility is also an important issue in human relationships. The question most of us ask is: "How can I develop compatibility with one and all?" We can adjust ourselves to be in sync with our spouse after thirty years of association, and with our children because as they grow up their samskaras manifest and we get used to one another. But with business partners at work, or in a school or college, there is an entire gamut of vibratory levels. Can we be in harmony with all of them at once? This happens only when we develop the empathy and acceptance to resonate with others, even when we do not agree with them. And these capacities are known as emotional intelligence (EQ) and social intelligence (SQ). They naturally develop with the expansion of consciousness that comes with spiritual practice.

Think of it like this: two people are climbing up a mountain, on opposite sides. The person climbing up the west slope can only see the west side of the mountain, and that colors her perception. The person climbing up the east side can only see the east, the opposite perspective. The two sides could be any duality: science versus religion, profit versus environmental sustainability in business, responsibility versus acceptance. Only when we reach the top of the mountain can we see both perspectives, integrate them into a 360-degree vision of the whole, and see all points of view. Only when our consciousness has expanded fully can we do this so that our vibrational levels are truly in harmony with everyone and everything in the universe.

Vibratory Level at Death

Earlier in the book, I mentioned that our destiny is not only associated with this physical dimension, but also with other dimensions—so what happens at the moment of death? Our vehicle, the physical body, is recycled back into the pool of atoms of matter, the five elements known as the *pancha bhutas*. Now what happens to the other two bodies, the subtle body and the soul? During any lifetime we create a vibratory blueprint that determines our onward destination, and at the moment of death our subtle bodies and soul go to the dimension that corresponds with that blueprint. They must match. The soul finds its level and its dimension according to the level of purity we have nurtured in the subtle bodies that envelop it and the potency of the soul. We determine this onward destination according to how we have lived our life on Earth. Some of us will come back again to a physical existence, because we have attached ourselves to people and things in this physical world that draw us back again. That is the play of our samskaras. Others of us will carry on to other subtler dimensions, where there is no need for a physical body. It all depends on the vibrational potency we have created during the life we have lived. There are many possibilities, but this topic is not within the scope of this book.

Some people ask: Can I purify myself at the moment of death so that my vibratory level is in tune with a very fine dimension? It doesn't work that way, because we cannot achieve something at the last moment. If we study a day before an exam, we may pass, but the outcome will be different if we prepare slowly from day one. Exams can happen any day. Death can happen any day, rather any moment. So to prepare ourselves to face the next dimension, it is good to remain in a very pure, fine vibratory level, and that is the vibration of love. It helps to have a lifestyle where we are always prepared for that last moment. Actually, it is not like the exam where we pass or fail, and this is not a reference to heaven and hell. It is a simple vibrational match: if my condition is very light, I will carry on to a lighter realm, whereas if I am carrying samskaric burdens, their weight will pull me back to the physical realm.

In addition to the work we do on ourselves, the Guide prepares us for this onward journey. Just as a mother gives birth to our physical entity into this physical world, a Guide of caliber can give birth to our Spiritual Entity into the higher dimensions known as the Brighter World. This is a very crucial step in the onward destiny of a seeker. The fascinating thing is that we remain alive here in this physical dimension while our Spiritual Entity is born into the Brighter World. Our Spiritual Entity can dwell in multiple dimensions. How do we understand this? Have you ever been in one place physically but thinking about somewhere else entirely? The mind is in another dimension, right? You may also be remembering someone you love dearly in the back of your mind, so your feeling is somewhere else again. We actually use our capacity to exist in multiple dimensions much more than we might think!

The functions of a mother and a true Guide are very similar. The mother nurtures the child within her womb for nine months before giving birth, and the Guide nurtures the spiritual child, the seeker, within his mental womb for some time. During this period, the seeker receives energy and nourishment from the spiritual waves of the Guide's thoughts. When the time is right, the seeker is born in the Brighter World, and his or her life commences in other dimensions.

When we are able to truly stay in the mental sphere of the Guide, surrendering everything to him, it takes only seven months for him to deliver us into the Brighter World, but the process is generally delayed because we are preoccupied with our own thoughts, feelings, and desires. If and when we are able to accept the Guide as a spiritual mother, the whole process becomes simple and natural, because we feel love and reverence for him, and naturally surrender just like a baby does to a mother.

But our relationship with the Guide generally does not start out with such a high level of acceptance and surrender. We may start by expecting to receive peace of mind, stillness, and a happy life, but eventually all of those things drop off, and we start accepting whatever comes very graciously. In one way, the role of the Guide is to help us accept life's situations with better understanding.

Just as there is tremendous joy when a mother delivers her baby into the physical world, there is also tremendous joy when the Guide delivers the seeker's Spiritual Entity into the Brighter World. The success of this delivery depends on our ability as seekers: it is not just the Guide's ability to retain the seeker, but also our ability to be retained in the Guide's mental womb due to immense love. Love is always for the sake of love, and the spiritual vacuum we create in our hearts pulls the flow of divine grace toward us.

At the time of our death, when the vehicle of the physical body expires, if we have a Spiritual Entity, it merges with the soul and subtle bodies. This mergence of the soul with the Spiritual Entity is called *mahasamadhi*. So the prerequisite for mahasamadhi is to have a Spiritual Entity. And the prerequisite for that is to build such a relationship with the Guide that we remain in his mental womb for at least seven months.

But there can be many other types of death and destinations after death, according to the vibratory blueprint we create during this life. Even among liberated souls, there are those who have a Spiritual Entity and those who do not have a Spiritual Entity in another dimension, because they do not have a living Guide who can create that Spiritual Entity, and so their deaths and their destinies will be different. Those souls that still carry a burden of samskaras in their subtle bodies will necessarily have to come back to this physical dimension, because of the weight of those impressions. This is not a punishment, just a simple fact that when we are attached to anything on the physical plane of existence, that attachment will pull us back here after death. That process is known as rebirth, which brings us to the next aspect of vibratory compatibility.

Vibratory Level at Conception

Now what happens at the beginning of the earthly journey, when we enter this world at the time of conception? What determines our parents, our place of birth, and the life we will lead here on earth?

Once I was visiting Chariji and I asked him, "Is the place of conception important? Is the time and place of delivery important?"

He replied, "None of these," and then said, "Think over it."

He then told us a story from the Mahabharata to give us a hint:

Raja Vichitravirya, the father of Dhritharashtra, Pandu, and Vidur, had two queens, but was unfortunately impotent. After his death, his mother wanted to ensure that he left behind a successor for the continuity of the royal lineage. An astrologer told her, "This is the perfect auspicious time. If the queens can conceive during the next two hours, the children will be of a glorious nature, worthy of a king's succession."

So she ordered her eldest son, who was a rishi, to come. He came immediately, unwashed, with mattered hair flowing and smelling unpleasant. He went to mate with the first queen, and when she saw him she was aghast and closed her eyes: "My

God! With this man I have to mate!" Disgusted, she said, "All right, if it is necessary, so let it be."

Likewise, when the rishi went to the second queen's chamber, she was frozen as if her blood circulation had completely stopped. Two children were conceived: the child born to the first queen was blind, and the child born to the second had pale, leucodermic skin. The condition of these children at birth was determined by the attitude of the queens at the moment of conception.

These two queens had also decided upon a backup plan in case they failed to conceive. They requested one of their maids to also mate with the rishi. The maid felt so proud, honored, thankful, and grateful to God for sending the rishi to give her a child, and her child was the wisest of the lot.

A beautiful idea emerged from this discussion with Chariji: it is the *attitude of the couple* at the moment of conception that matters. At the moment of conception, not just any soul, but a soul with the corresponding vibratory level matching with the future parents, will descend into the womb that has the specific vibratory level. It will match. It is like iron filings drawn to a magnet—it is a natural process where the vibratory blueprint of a particular soul will be attracted to the blueprint offered by the parents. The attitude of the parents will make all the difference. It is like lock and key. So you are deciding the destiny of your family at that time. And can you manufacture a super fine vibratory level at that moment? No. At the moment of conception you cannot fabricate it just because you want a Jesus Christ or a Vivekananda in your family. The preparation has to be done years ahead.

Once the soul has descended, it is too late to manipulate the time of birth by Caesarean section to try for a particular destiny according to astrology. The baby already has the baggage of its own samskaras. How does it matter afterward when these samskaras unfold? So the time of birth is not important in itself, because the load of samskara is already there. The soul that will be embodied and delivered is already there.

Vibratory Level and Meditation

Just as we take birth according to the vibratory level of our parents, likewise, when we sit to meditate, we prepare the canvas of our vibratory field to receive a spiritual condition. What is that state of consciousness? Take a minute to think about the canvas you create in the morning when you meditate. What is your attitude? Are you thinking, "Is my mother watching to see if I have my eyes closed?" And what happens when you are rushing, when you need to finish meditation quickly to get ready for college or work? Perhaps you really want to meditate with all your heart, but you are really pressed for time. What sort of creative condition will come?

At least those two queens in the Mahabharata could conceive one blind child and one weak child. Will you be able to create any condition? Not if you meditate half-heartedly or in a rush. And, sometimes, a wonderful condition is created, but it is aborted, as in the early days of pregnancy. This happens when you are careless about your lifestyle. You meditate so beautifully, and then straight away you go out into the world without imbibing your condition, and there goes your condition.

Now contrast those scenarios with one where you go to bed in a prayerful condition, sleeping with the longing that you will wake up early to meet your beloved in meditation with so much love in your heart. You wake early, refreshed, with a heart full of love and intense longing. What is the state of your consciousness now? What sort of canvas have you created to receive a spiritual condition? Then you meditate, acquire the condition, and take time to enliven it, imbibe it, become one with it, and merge with it.

Take Interest

So the key is to take interest in how you conduct your life, because that is what destiny is all about. Kahlil Gibran wrote in his book, *The Prophet,* "Work is love made visible. And if you cannot work with love but only with distaste, it is better that you should leave your work and sit at the gate of the temple and take alms of those who work with joy." It is the same with meditation. Do it with love; do it with interest. Poise, focus, and enthusiasm go a long way in creating the right vibratory field for us to design our destiny. It does not take much to change the trajectory of a life—in fact, it is as simple as turning our head from one side to the other.

I think a lot depends on what we really want. We will certainly find time for things that interest us. For things that do not interest us, even if we have the time we will run away from them. So it is not a matter of finding time. Do we have the interest? If we do, then we will find the time. Success in spirituality, as in education, career, or any other field, depends upon three principles:

Do you really want it? Are you interested?
Are you committed?
What are you doing for it?

If our lives are governed by these three principles, I think we will easily bring forward the lofty goal of absolute balance and enlightenment into the here and now.

At the same time, the evolution of our consciousness will help us perform our duties and actions so well that people will be amazed at every little thing we do, be it in business, studies or family life. This perfection will slowly percolate into our relationships and career. So even at a worldly level, it is worth investing our emotional energies into meditation so that we don't lose our balance.

And there are many other reasons to meditate even after we reach that lofty height of spirituality. Not only will we achieve the goal for ourselves, we can then meditate for others. Whenever we meditate and think of someone else, that person in some miraculous way is also affected by our condition. And when another person is thinking of us when we meditate, automatically our consciousness touches their hearts. They also feel at ease, at peace. So our meditation not only brings a revolution in our own hearts and so much peace and tranquility, it also helps others who are not actively meditating by the simple fact that they are associated with us in some way.

One day, I was asking some young people a question: "How long is the spiritual journey?"

One person answered very brilliantly, "The blink of an eye."

That means we can achieve the highest within a fraction of a second.

Another person said, "It is infinite, never ending."

Both are right. We expand infinitely with love and contract infinitely into that zero state with the blink of an eye and are totally gone within. That is also infinity. This contraction and expansion is a constant process in which we expand with love and contract into insignificance. This exercise should go on.

Our soul is craving something really magnificent. It is craving that ultimate state of oneness we call Samadhi in Yoga, which means "that which prevailed before the creation came into existence." Samadhi is considered to be the goal of Yoga, an inner experience of purity and balance that is one with the original state. During our yogic practice, we also encounter various stages or glimpses of Samadhi as we progress on the journey toward this original state. Samadhi is the ultimate spiritual relaxation and the ultimate effortless concentration, and it is considered to be the goal of human existence in Yoga.

Unless and until we achieve that absolute balance within, the soul will always find some sort of shortcoming in anything we do in life. When we achieve the Samadhi state in all our activities, both worldly and spiritual, then true happiness will come on its own, even at those times when we seem to fail in our actions in the worldly sense. We will remain unshaken. Try to invite such states of Samadhi day after day and make them permanent. That is the Heartfulness way.

I wish you all the best in this grand adventure of evolution and destiny, and hope to join you as a fellow traveler on this magnificent journey toward the ultimate destination.

GLOSSARY

ahankar: Identity, ego, and will. One of the four main subtle bodies.

antakaran: The inner being, the inner cause or origin of thought and feeling. The word originates from the Sanskrit *antar*.

Ashtanga Yoga: Patanjali's description of Yoga made up of eight limbs or steps: *Yama, Niyama, Asana, Pranayama, Pratyahara, Dharana, Dhyana,* and *Samadhi.*

Asana: Aligning posture. The third limb of Patanjali's Ashtanga Yoga.

buddhi: The mind's discriminating instrument, intellect, and intelligence. It evolves to encompass intuition, wisdom, and higher ignorance. One of the four main subtle bodies.

Chandra Nadi: One of the three main energy channels in the body, associated with the moon, the parasympathetic nervous system, the left nostril for breathing, the left side of the body, rest, and sleep. Is also called the *Ida Nadi.*

chit: Consciousness. It is one of the four main subtle bodies, which is purified and expands as we evolve.

Dharana: Aligning thoughts, the flow of intention, inward. The sixth limb of Patanjali's Ashtanga Yoga.

Dhyana: Regulating the mind and expanding the spectrum of consciousness to reach the Center. The seventh limb of Patanjali's Ashtanga Yoga.

egregore: A collective thought-form, feeling-form, or vibrational field. It is created by our collective thoughts and feelings. It creates an atmosphere.

Ekadashi: The eleventh day after each full moon and new moon in the lunar cycle, which is generally observed as a day of fasting in the Hindu calendar.

ghazal: A form of amatory poetry, an ode, often sung, expressing the beauty of love and the pain of separation from the Beloved.

gunas: The three qualities of nature in Indian schools of philosophy: *sat, raj,* and *tam.*

Guru: One who transmits light or knowledge; a spiritual teacher.

gurukula: The ancient Indian system of education where students live with the Guru.

Ida: The *Nadi* or subtle current starting and ending on the left side of the spinal cord, associated with the moon and the parasympathetic nervous system. See *Chandra Nadi.*

japa: Remembrance of God, often in the form of the repetition of the name of God or a mantra.

jnana, gyan, gyana: Knowledge; the ability to think, reflect, and exhibit good behavior.

Jnana Yoga: The path or aspect of Yoga associated with knowledge and wisdom. Jnana Yoga is the practical realization of the condition prevailing at each chakra on the spiritual journey.

karana sharir: Causal body, or soul. It is the cause of the subtle and physical bodies. It contains the seeds of all the formations of the sensory and motor organs and the mind.

karma: Action. Results of actions or fruits of actions are also called karma.

Kena Upanishad: One of the primary Upanishads, it is a Vedic Sanskrit text notable for its discussion of Brahman with and without attributes, and a treatise on pure knowledge.

Mahabharata: Great epic war in Indian history, involving the Pandavas, Kauravas, and Lord Krishna.

mahasamadhi: The final Samadhi when an evolved soul leaves the body and merges with the Spiritual Entity in the Brighter World.

manas: Mind. Also the name of one of the four main subtle bodies, contemplative thinking, and feeling function.

mantra: A sound, sometimes repeated, particularly a sacred sound, word, or phrase.

Nirvana: A transcendent state in which there is neither suffering, desire, nor a sense of self, and the subject is released from the effects of karma and the cycle of death and rebirth. It represents the final goal of Buddhism.

Niyama: Refining behavior by cultivating noble qualities. The second limb of Patanjali's Ashtanga Yoga.

pancha bhutas: The five ancient elements of nature: earth, water, fire, air, and ether. Each of the chakras within the Heart Region is dominated by one of these elements—chakra 1 by earth, chakra 2 by ether, chakra 3 by fire, chakra 4 by water and chakra 5 by air.

Pingala: The *Nadi* or subtle current starting and ending on the right side of the spinal cord, associated with the sun and the sympathetic nervous system. See *Surya Nadi.*

prana: Energy, life, breath.

pranahuti: Yogic transmission. Derived from *prana*, meaning life, and *ahuti*, meaning offering. Offering of the life force from the Guru's heart into the disciple's heart.

pranasya prana: Literally "life in life." A term used in the *Kena Upanishad* to describe pranahuti.

Pranayama: Refining the energy body—aligning energy and breath. The fourth limb of Patanjali's Ashtanga Yoga.

Pratyahara: Refining the attention—aligning the senses inward. The fifth limb of Patanjali's Ashtanga Yoga.

rajasic: Pertaining to and promoting *raj*, one of the three gunas, associated with activity and desires.

sahaj: Means "natural." Sahaj Samadhi is natural Samadhi, for example, where a person is in the original state of balance while also completely alert and active in the world, with 360-degree consciousness.

Samadhi: Original balance. Realizing nonbeing—the absolute state of balance at the Center. The eighth limb of Patanjali's Ashtanga Yoga and the culmination of yogic practice.

samskara: Impression.

sankalpa: Subtle, prayerful suggestion backed by intention.

sat-chit-anand: Existence-consciousness-bliss. The state associated with *Sahasra-Dal-Kamal*, the thousand-petaled lotus.

sattvik: Pertaining to *sat*, one of the three *gunas* that promotes peace, calmness, nobility.

shastra: Holy book, scripture.

sloka: A verse.

sookshma sharir: The subtle body, astral body, or heart-mind.

sthoola sharir: Physical body.

Surya Nadi: One of the three main energy channels in the body, associated with the sun, the sympathetic nervous system, the right nostril for breathing, the right side of the body, and activity. It is also called the *Pingala Nadi*.

Surya Namaskar: A series of graceful Asanas practiced to salute the sun.

Sushumna Nadi: The central *Nadi* in the body, running straight up the spinal cord. It is the central channel for the flow of prana, associated with balance and symmetry.

sushupti: One of the four states of consciousness. It is described as the consciousness of deep sleep in which a man does not dream. When this state of mind is attained, a man gets in close communion with God, though he remains in a forgetful state.

tamasic: Pertaining to and promoting *tam*, one of the three *gunas*, associated with inertness, laziness, dullness, and procrastination.

tavajjo: Means "attention"; the Farsi equivalent of Transmission, or pranahuti.

Turiya: Fourth state. The other three states are: *jagrat*—waking state; *swapna*—dream state; sushupti—deep sleep state.

Turiyatit: Beyond the Turiya condition, where the soul becomes one with God and the Turiya condition expands into daily life.

Vairagya: Detachment, renunciation.

vayu: Air, air principle.

Yama: Refining behavior—removing unwanted habits. The first limb of Patanjali's Ashtanga Yoga.

Yoga: Means "union, joining." The practices and philosophy leading to the union of the lower self with the Higher Self or God.

Yoga Sutras: A treatise describing the principles of Yoga, containing 196 sutras written by the great sage, Patanjali. Notably, it introduces the eight limbs of Ashtanga Yoga.

RECOMMENDED READING

Heartfulness Literature

The Heartfulness Way: Heart-Based Meditations for Spiritual Transformation, by Kamlesh D. Patel and Joshua Pollock

Complete Works of Ram Chandra, Volumes 1 to 6, by Ram Chandra

Reality at Dawn, by Ram Chandra (also in Volume 1 of the *Complete Works*)

Efficacy of Raja Yoga in the Light of Sahaj Marg, by Ram Chandra (also in Volume 1 of the *Complete Works*)

Towards Infinity, by Ram Chandra (also in Volume 1 of the *Complete Works*)

Other Recommended Books

Complete Works of Swami Vivekananda, Volumes 1 to 9, by Swami Vivekananda

Emotional Intelligence: Why It Can Matter More than IQ, by Daniel Goleman

The Biology of Belief: Unleashing the Power of Consciousness, Matter & Miracles, by Dr. Bruce Lipton

The Songs of Trees: Stories from Nature's Great Connectors, by David George Haskell

ABOUT HEARTFULNESS

Heartfulness is a heart-centered approach to life. It is to live naturally, in accordance with the qualities and attitudes of a heart enlightened and refined through spiritual practice. This includes qualities such as compassion, kindness, empathy, sincerity, contentment, truthfulness, and forgiveness; attitudes such as generosity and acceptance; and the heart's fundamental nature, which is love. The Heartfulness approach to life is supported by four basic practices for beginners. From the very first day, these practices start revealing these qualities in us.

Heartfulness is a system of Raja-Yoga meditation that emerged out of Northern India a century ago. Over time it was simplified and distilled into the practices we know today, which are available through the Heartfulness Institute. Heartfulness Centers exist in 140 countries, and there are currently over 13,000 certified trainers offering meditation sessions free of charge to all who are interested to learn and master the practices.

Experience Heartfulness Firsthand

Heartfulness Institute US website: www.heartfulness.org
Heartfulness Institute UK website: www.heartfulness.uk

Download the HeartsApp for Android and iOS to contact a trainer, to schedule classes, and for access to guided practices, classes, and online meditation sessions.

Contact a trainer in one of our centers, known as HeartSpots, at https://heartspots.heartfulness.org.

Follow the three introductory masterclasses online at https://heartfulness.org/en/masterclass.

Connect with the Heartfulness Institute:
On Facebook: www.facebook.com/practiceheartfulness
On Twitter: @heartful_ness
On Instagram: @heartfulness

Connect with Daaji:
Daaji's website: www.daaji.org
On Facebook: www.facebook.com/kamleshdaaji
On Twitter: @kamleshdaaji
On Instagram: @kamleshdaaji

Read the Heartfulness Magazine: www.heartfulnessmagazine.com

ABOUT THE AUTHOR

Known widely as **Daaji, Kamlesh D. Patel** has been a student of spirituality all his life. He is interested in sharing his learnings from his personal experience on the path of Heartfulness, while reflecting his deep spirit of inquiry and respect for the world's great spiritual traditions and scientific advancements.

Daaji practiced pharmacy in New York City for over three decades before being named the successor in a century-old lineage of spiritual masters. He is the fourth and current Heartfulness Guide, fulfilling the many duties of a modern-day teacher of yogic meditation and purposeful living.

Today he extends his support to spiritual seekers everywhere, sharing yogic Transmission with one and all, so that even novices can experience the effects of meditation. This Transmission is a special feature of Heartfulness, which makes this system so effective. He also devotes much of his time and energy to research in the field of consciousness and spirituality, approaching the subject with scientific methodology—a practical approach that stems from his own experience and mastery in the field.

Connect with him and the Heartfulness Institute at www.heartfulness.org and www.daaji.org.

We hope you enjoyed this Hay House book. If you'd like to receive our online catalog featuring additional information on Hay House books and products, or if you'd like to find out more about the Hay Foundation, please contact:

Hay House, Inc., P.O. Box 5100, Carlsbad, CA 92018-5100
(760) 431-7695 or (800) 654-5126
(760) 431-6948 (fax) or (800) 650-5115 (fax)
www.hayhouse.com® • www.hayfoundation.org

———

Published in Australia by: Hay House Australia Pty. Ltd.,
18/36 Ralph St., Alexandria NSW 2015
Phone: 612-9669-4299 • *Fax:* 612-9669-4144
www.hayhouse.com.au

Published in the United Kingdom by: Hay House UK, Ltd.,
The Sixth Floor, Watson House, 54 Baker Street, London W1U 7BU
Phone: +44 (0)20 3927 7290 • *Fax:* +44 (0)20 3927 7291
www.hayhouse.co.uk

Published in India by: Hay House Publishers India,
Muskaan Complex, Plot No. 3, B-2, Vasant Kunj, New Delhi 110 070
Phone: 91-11-4176-1620 • *Fax:* 91-11-4176-1630
www.hayhouse.co.in

———

Access New Knowledge.
Anytime. Anywhere.

Learn and evolve at your own pace
with the world's leading experts.

www.hayhouseU.com

Hay House Podcasts
Bring Fresh, Free Inspiration Each Week!

Hay House proudly offers a selection of life-changing audio content via our most popular podcasts!

Hay House Meditations Podcast

Features your favorite Hay House authors guiding you through meditations designed to help you relax and rejuvenate. Take their words into your soul and cruise through the week!

Dr. Wayne W. Dyer Podcast

Discover the timeless wisdom of Dr. Wayne W. Dyer, world-renowned spiritual teacher and affectionately known as "the father of motivation." Each week brings some of the best selections from the 10-year span of Dr. Dyer's talk show on Hay House Radio.

Hay House Podcast

Enjoy a selection of insightful and inspiring lectures from Hay House Live events, listen to some of the best moments from previous Hay House Radio episodes, and tune in for exclusive interviews and behind-the-scenes audio segments featuring leading experts in the fields of alternative health, self-development, intuitive medicine, success, and more! Get motivated to live your best life possible by subscribing to the free Hay House Podcast.

Find Hay House podcasts on iTunes, or visit
www.HayHouse.com/podcasts for more info.